Things I Wish My Parents Taught Me

REAL LIFE LESSONS FOR ACQUIRING SUCCESS

Bruce Ellemo

Published by Prominence Publishing.
For information, visit www.prominencepublishing.com

Cover photography by Gordon Clark Photography. For information, visit http://gordonclarkphotography.com.

Bruce Ellemo can be reached at www.BruceEllemo.com.

ISBN: 978-0-9958775-0-4
First Edition: June 2017

TABLE OF CONTENTS

PROLOGUE

I started to write this book primarily for my children. I wanted to make sure that I was able to pass down to them the things I learned from my parents, my readings and my life. I wanted my children to learn from my successes and failures. From that initial goal, it transcended into a book that included my own summaries from some of the world's great thinkers, and my own understandings of life.

While my parents did their best to teach us 'what life is all about,' their only resource was themselves and, in turn, what they had learned from their own parents. This is, of course, the same for many of us. The problem with this is that, if we only know what our parents taught us, and so on down the family line of the generations, we become a product of past generations without knowing why – or even realizing it. We also grow up with no real idea about how to change that path, either, should we want to.

I am certain that there was all sorts of good information and habits that were passed down to me through the generations before me. But at the end of the day, I am the only person who can decide what is good from me or not. I am the only person who can decide who I am and who I can become. It was upon making this realization that I started to read books on self-development and personal growth in attempt to find information for new, outside sources.

I kept asking myself, "How do I get more happiness, more love, more money, more satisfaction, more strength, more health and how do I become a better person?" The first book of this nature that I read, when I was 18 years old, was Norman Vincent Peale's *The Power of Positive Thinking*. This type of material really resonated with me and it created for me a lifetime of interest in reading books from leaders in this field, including but not limited to Earl Nightingale, James Allen, Eckhart Tolle, Stephen Covey and the legendary Mr. Bob Proctor. Bob has had a real impact on my life that I am eternally grateful for.

I had fantastic parents who are very loving and gave everything they had to us in terms of love, money and time. My father, Norm, was very active in the community, coaching us in all of our sports, while my mother preferred to read and enjoy the quieter things in life. My father was the most positive-thinking man I had ever known and still know to this day. I am very fortunate to have his optimism and positive attitude ingrained in me. My mother has blessed me with compassion, kindness and a calmness that I am also grateful for.

Life was pretty good – some might say easy - for me up until I left my family home at 20 years old. After I left home I began to learn life's lessons the hard way, as most of us do - by making mistakes. My crash-course to life was beginning and I didn't even know it. From my understanding, this is the only way it can be done; you must make mistakes before you have your breakthrough.

Believe me, there have been plenty of bumps along the way – some larger than others.

I have gone from living in an abandoned theatre in one of the roughest neighbourhoods in Vancouver, to having a million-dollar house in upper-class suburban neighbourhood. I have gone from driving a $2,000 car to driving a $60,000 car.

During my university days, I had a great job at the City of Victoria from which I was fired. In fact, I was actually fired from every job I ever had. I wasn't suited to be led by others, I am suited to lead. I have gone from being single, to being married for 20 years, to being single again. I built a very successful equipment-lease company only to have my ex-brother and sister-in-law try to take it from me in a frivolous lawsuit. The business remains mine today.

Many of these situations were difficult, but I could not be more thankful for them, as they gave me the successes and failures upon which I built my life. The negative experiences helped me to better understand myself, my life and the people in it. I can assure you that what feels like failure will teach you 100 times more about yourself than victory does. My failures have afforded me opportunities to test my will and to gain mental toughness and emotional resilience. I learned how the mind works. I have gone through enough of life's paces that it would be very difficult to unhinge me anymore. My past has given me the ability to write this book for which I am very grateful.

I really want to convey to you, through the course of this book, that the game of life is played between your ears. Life is, quite simply, a culmination of your thoughts and perceptions about your circumstances. It is about your ability to get a clear idea of who you are and what you want. And then, it's about your ability to set the course in order to achieve what you want. Life exists and is played out in the mind. Your perception of your life can be changed with a simple change of your thought processes. This is free and attainable to all who challenge it.

After having read hundreds of books over the past 30 years, and since finding my passion in personal development, it has become clear to me that there are specific life activities and belief systems that will give you your best life. There are specific activities and ways of thinking that will help you create the best well-rounded version of yourself. Life isn't that complicated, and if we can slow ourselves down and be disciplined, life can be the truly magical event that it is supposed to be. Life is meant to be fun, exciting, full of passion, love, wealth, health, peace and enjoyment. We are supposed to dream big, work hard and accomplish a lot. We are meant to reach our destiny and be fulfilled.

It's just too bad how often things don't work out that way. We often underperform and underachieve. We are often not reaching or learning to be our best selves. We often do not have the best life possible. Too often, we are unfulfilled. I learned this firsthand, after experience a number of challenges and the ups and downs of my life. I have studied myself as well as others, for the last three decades, looking for a pattern of thoughts, beliefs and activities that will ensure we are at peace in our hearts and minds. Patterns that will assure us that we are satiated with what we have, while working towards the things in our minds that we want and search for. These patterns will help you develop your passions in life, they will resurrect a state of peaceful being that will serve as the foundation of your life. It is these patterns, behaviours and the disciplines in this book, that serve as either a reaffirmation that you are on track or a launching pad to develop the best possible you.

As humans, we are very unique. However, at our core, we are all essentially the same. We all generally want the same things in life, sometimes to varying degrees. That is to say that we all want abundance in the areas of health, money, love, friendships, leisure, peace, joy, spirituality, and purpose. We want to leave a legacy for the ones we love and for the world at large.

Having been on the planet for almost half a century has given me opportunities to succeed and fail at almost everything I have tried. I have failed hundreds of times and through this have also ended up with tremendous successes, too. All of these successes and failures have taught me a tried, tested and true behavioural system that can save years, even decades of wasted time and grief. There are very common threads amongst us that exists as responses to life and its failures and successes. I hope to pass those thoughts on to others.

You can learn to unlock the magic in your life. The pages of this book contain a plan, or path, that has been used by myself, and by millions of others, that will lead you to being your 'best you' possible.

I am often asked why we don't always reach that pinnacle of being the "best person" we can be. Well, I'll take the kid gloves off and tell you bluntly - it's primarily because we don't work at it. If you want to learn the play the piano, you have to practice daily and play consistently for many years. If you want to be a gymnast, you must work at gymnastics for many years. If you want to live your best life, you will need to work at it in the same fashion. Yes, it seems like a long time, and it is, but the rewards are tremendous. Whether you are 10 years old or 70 years old, if you are not living a life where happiness surrounds in all your endeavours, then it's time to embark on a new journey.

Happiness is found inside. You don't have to turn your whole world upside down, you simply need to start looking at life with a different perspective, a different attitude, and a different slant. You need to have laser focus on who you are and what you want in the future. As humans we are designed to grow, to always be expanding and to want more.

You don't need to look anywhere else for the best you, you don't have to have any material items to be the best you. You have been designed to perfection, whoever you are. You have all that you have ever needed inside you right now, you simply have to engage in daily habits and ways of thinking that will propel you to be your best. It won't be easy and will take time, discipline, repetition and consistency. You see, it is consistency that will yield results.

I have had a fantastic journey working on myself, trying things to see how the results turn out. There have been failures and great successes. There are things that have worked and things that haven't.

The purpose of this book is to give you direction and provide a springboard to finding success, and to become the absolute best person you can be. Success comes in many forms and is based in how we perceive success.

Define what success means to you. You must know what success means to you before you get going. The meaning of success is different for all of us. If you don't know what success means to you then you will have no way to get there. It would be the same as planning a vacation but not knowing where you want to go. Create a plan that will generate a path towards your definition of success and be consistent in the daily behaviours that will take you there.

It is way easier than you think, you just need to be disciplined and understand the effect that repetition has on the outcome of your life. Have fun with it, laugh at your failures, and laugh even harder at your successes. But do yourself a favour and enjoy the ride because it is meant to be spectacular.

CHAPTER 1

FALSE BILL OF SALE

At some point along the way, I believe we will look back at the way our children were raised in the school environment and how we raised our children at home and ask our selves some serious questions. Don't get me wrong, I think we are doing a good enough job – and on the home front, my parents were, and still are, wonderful – but since when is 'good enough' our goal? Our children, our leaders of the future, deserve more. I think, down the road, we will question the subjects that our children were taught in school as much as we will question the people who taught them. We will question some of the principles, ideas and concepts that we taught our children as they grew. You see, as we grew up, we were sold a false bill of sale. As children we were steered and built by our parents, our school system and teachers within that system. A child's life is like a piece of paper in which every person leaves a mark.

What differentiates us from animals is that we can think, reason and be creative. I have had the good fortune of meeting Mr. Bob Proctor and his business partner, Ms. Sandy Gallagher. Bob writes "When squirrels are born they can immediately climb a tree, scamper around and survive on their own. They can fend for themselves. We are totally disoriented in ours. Why? Because even though we've been given the mental faculty to create our own environment, we don't do it. The squirrel is completely home in its environment. When humans are born we are completely helpless and need constant care in order to survive otherwise we die."[1]

As young and impressionable children, the message many of us received from our parents was to take risks, keep going, and not worry about falling down. Yes, they said, you may get hurt and skin a knee but it's not the end of the world. We had to fall down in order to learn to walk. We made incoherent noises before we learned to speak. We smiled before we laughed and we had to eat baby food before we ate meat. There is a natural order to the way we learn and grow as children.

Up to a certain point, children are completely creative and use their imagination to its fullest. That is until we get to school. This is when we change, and begin – whether we know it or not - to start thinking inside the box of the school system. Yes, we need to know math, science and a certain set of skills required to move forward in the world. However, our creativity is often shut down inside the walls of these classrooms. A child only needs to hear things like "That is silly,"; "Grow up,"; "Don't do it that way,"; "Be quiet,"; "Who do you think you are?"; "Don't color outside the lines," a few times before they start to lose confidence in their own ideas. It stifles creativity, even if those providing the "lesson" mean well.

---

[1] Proctor, B., & Gallagher, S. (2016). *The art of living*. New York City: Tarcher.

Well, why don't children just ignore that way of thinking? Well, that's easier said than done because children are very impressionable. Their beliefs about themselves and the world are shaped by the adults that surround them daily. What has propelled us through time is our resilience and determination. A child learns to walk by falling a multitude of times. He never gives up, thinking to himself, "Maybe this isn't for me." When you are a child in school and you become restless, wanting to move around or speak your mind, you're told to settle down, stop what you're doing and quit disrupting the class. Who says we can't do it that way? Our teachers, parents and friends tell us we can't do things, or that it will be too hard. These messages are discouraging and not helpful in the long run.

The message we should be telling our children instead is that it is important for them to find their own ways to do things. We should be encouraging them to try things whichever way they want in order to eventually figure out what works. You see, once you make all the necessary mistakes you will know what not to do the next time. Eventually, you'll figure it out, and you'll be better for it having done it on your own.

As we age, we become totally disoriented in our own environment. We are no longer like the squirrel scrambling around with agility and confidence. We are no longer like a horse that is running within weeks of birth. We become and grow into the mixed bag of contrasting beliefs that were taught by our parents our teachers and others in our circle of influence at the time. First, we are taught to take risks, fall down and not worry because this is how you learn to walk and live. Once we get to a certain age we are taught and told things that suggest we should conform, play it safe, and be more like others.

A shift starts to take place that takes us away from a risk-taking mentality to a more cautious and careful mentality. This is the first step that begins to disconnect us from our potential. This is the beginning of limited growth.

Did you know the school curriculum in Finland revolves around the children having little to no homework? They are encouraged to play for most of the day. The main goal for the children is to make sure they are enjoying themselves. The teachers follow the children around all day and continuously ask them if they are having fun. They want these children to use their imaginations as much as possible and to not shut down their creative spirit. These minds that are so brilliant, and yet underused. Did you also know that Finnish schools have the highest marks of all schools and that these children go on to be among the happiest and most fulfilled adults? Did you know that Finland is at the top of the charts for the best places in the world to live?

That can't just be one big coincidence, can it?

The transformation of the Finnish education system began some 40 years ago as the key propellant of the country's economic recovery plan. Educators had little idea it would be so successful until 2000 when the first results from the program for International Student Assessment (PISA), a standardized test given to 15-year-olds in more than 40 global venues, revealed Finnish youth to be the best young readers in the world. Three years later, they were leading in math as well. By 2006, Finland was first out of 57 countries in science. In the 2009 PISA scores, the nation came in second in science, third in reading and sixth in math among nearly half a million students worldwide. "I'm still surprised," said Arjariita Heikkinen, principal of a Helsinki comprehensive school, "I didn't realize we were that good."

There are no mandated standardized tests in Finland either, apart from one exam at the end of students' senior year in high school. There are no rankings, no comparisons or competition between students, schools or regions. Finland's schools are all publicly funded. The people in the government agencies running them, from national officials to local authorities, are educators, not business people, military leaders or career politicians. Every school has the same national goals and draws from the same pool of university-trained educators. The result is that a Finnish child will receive the same quality education no matter whether he or she lives in a rural village or a university town. All told, 93 percent of Finns graduate from academic or vocational high schools with grades that are 17.5 percentage points higher than the United States, and 66 percent go on to higher education, the highest rate in the European Union. Yet, Finland spends about 30 percent less per student than does the United States.

Teachers in Finland spend fewer hours at school each day and less total time in classrooms than American teachers. Teachers use the extra time to build curriculum and assess students. Children spend far more time playing outside, even in the depths of winter. Homework is minimal. Compulsory schooling does not begin until age seven. "We have no hurry," said Louhivuori, "Children learn better when they are ready, why stress them out?" North American parents often have other ideas, myself included. We want to enroll little Johnny into hockey at four years old and have him training four to five days a week by eight years old. We do this so he will have a chance to be the next professional hockey player. Let's put Cindy in dance, soccer, piano, pre-kindergarten education and singing by the time she is seven.

Sure, it would be wonderful if Johnny enjoys hockey, doesn't get burned out from it, and goes on to be the next Gordie Howe or Wayne Gretzky. And wouldn't it be wonderful if Cindy goes on to a long career as a Hollywood actress or Grammy-award winner or Olympic soccer player? Of course it would. But really, what are the odds? Slim.

In many cases, this method is too competitive and often backfires. Instead, let kids be kids.

In Finland, it's almost unheard of for a child to show up to school hungry, let alone be homeless. Finland provides three years of maternity leave, subsidized daycare, and preschool for all five-year-olds. At preschool, the emphasis is, you guessed it, on play and socializing. In addition, the state subsidizes parents, paying them around 150 euros per month for every child until he or she turns 17. As well, 97 percent of all 6-year-olds attend public preschool, where children begin some academic learning. Schools provide food, medical care, counseling and taxi service, if needed. Student health care is free.

Our school system – and many others in the Western world - teaches children how to conform and to be prepared for certain employment down the road. We are taught that once we achieve this employment or goal of making money we will be happy and satisfied.

I am here to tell you it should be the other way around. We should be taught to be happy and creative. We should be taught how to be satisfied and to not have to compete against the world in order to find our happiness. If we were taught this way, we would more easily find the passion that would allow us to make a personally meaningful living in this world. At school, we should be taught to figure it out on our own. This is the foundation of the Finnish school curriculum. Children are encouraged to find out what it is like to climb a tree, to fall off the monkey bars, and also to be silent for period of time. Allowing children to play with no boundaries, no preconceived ideas, encouraging them to think creatively and to make mistakes gives them the opportunities to figure it out on their own. It prepares them for real life in different ways than our schools do. What happens when children don't have peace of mind, joy and happiness? Usually, they become adults who don't have peace of mind, joy and happiness. We as adults have to "relearn" a lot of things. Most of us aren't capable, or simply don't want to spend the time relearning how to have these things.

We need to be taught how to be peaceful, happy and creative as the foundation of our being and our future. Our future selves can be most productive and creative once we are peaceful, happy and internally fulfilled.

In spite of having marvelous minds, many of us struggle and think they we are simply stuck with the circumstances that surrounded us. We shrug our shoulders and say things like, "I'd love to do it but I can't because…." Whatever follows "because" is the circumstance that we become slaves to. The circumstance becomes our "truth" and we react to our perceptions of the circumstance. We often don't even try to come up with a new, potentially better, way of dealing with it.

If there is one thing I hear more than anything else it is, "I can't do it." My response often is "Have you tried?" The answers "No", or "I did but it didn't work" are the typical replies. We can do whatever it is we want, we just need to have the proper mindset and a game plan, combined with perseverance, discipline and repetition. When you go on to do things in life you have never done, there may be a voice in your head that says "Who do you think you are? you can't do that. You can't possibly write a book, complete that triathlon, make $1,000,000 per year or whatever it is you are thinking of doing." This will turn into a mental battle and more often than not the little voice will win the conversation.

There is a strange thing that happens in our minds as a result of fear. A little voice says, "What if I don't succeed? What will people think when I fail?" Or we may think, "I don't have the skills to do this." As a result, we don't even begin to try. Legendary football coach Don Shula has been known to say that it is the start that stops most people. He is absolutely right.

The little voice goes on to justify the lack of action by telling us that it probably wouldn't have worked anyway, or that it wasn't the best idea for whatever reason, in spite of the fact that we probably would have loved to do it. The little voice tells us that it will be too much work, too costly, too time consuming, or "fill in the blank". These are called excuses; they are the things we tell ourselves as to why we are not getting what we want out of life. These are the stories we tell our family, friends and the world at large. Our brain will tell us whatever it needs to in order to prevent us from acting on the wants and desires that bring us greatness. Our brain will talk us out of changing that habit, taking that risk, going for it, living life on your terms. Do yourself a favour and don't miss out on experiencing passion in your life because a little voice that tells you that you can't do it. It can be done. All you need is the will, a plan, discipline and time.

I remember a couple of years ago, a little voice told me that I could not complete a 140-km ride on a bike. Knowing what I know about the mind and how success breeds success, I bought a bike and rode that distance in Ryder Hyjedal's Tour de Victoria bike race. I didn't start training by biking 140 km, of course. It was a little bit every day and a little bit more the next day until four months later I was fit to ride the race. The following year, I thought I might do a triathlon. Immediately the little voice said "I can't do that it is too hard, it will be too much training, I don't have the time." Instead of giving in, I made a plan to train and completed the Subaru triathlon. The year following that, I said to myself, "I have been reading hundreds of books and so why don't I write a book?" Guess what the little voice told me? "You can't write a book, it's too hard, you've never done it, it will take forever and besides, you're not an author." I immediately set out a plan to write this book. For one hour every morning for eight months, I worked on this book while sitting at my local Starbucks. Now, I have a book with my name on it.

If you let the little voice inside your head beat you into never even beginning, then you are giving yourself permission to not challenge yourself. As a result, you will not achieve what you desire. Not starting something you are passionate about, or want to try, provides nothing but negative momentum and gives you an escape for next time. No matter how big or small, the next time you think about doing something new, simply go do it. Make a plan, figure out how long it will take and like Nike says, "Just do it." There will never be a good time and there will always be a boat load of excuses. You must overcome them all, so that the universal law of 'success breeds success' can flow freely in your life. It doesn't matter how big or small the goal, just make it happen.

I really like how Proctor explained this theory. He said that in order to figure out how to change his life, he didn't have to study anyone else's personality to show them how to change. He just had to look at his own. In other words, I don't have to study you; I just have to study me. We are all the same. The only difference is in appearances, and the truth is rarely in the appearance of things. Use your higher faculties and look within to create the life you want.

We have all been blessed, to varying degrees, with will, intuition, perception, emotion, memory, reason, and imagination. Developing these faculties allows us to control the outside world and not let it control us. What we begin to do is respond and not react. We must become the true stewards of our spirit and our life.

Einstein was right when he said, "The intuitive mind is a sacred gift and the rational mind is a faithful servant. We have created a society that honours the servant and has forgotten the gift." What we need to do is gather an understanding of how we were programed from childhood, by our teachers and our parents. Next we need to know how we can change so that programming stops controlling us and we start controlling ourselves. That's when the fun starts and you become your own master. Only then can you truly let go of what other people think. Most of us seem to care about what other people think, but it is not worth your time. In fact, regardless of what you think, other people are likely not as concerned with you as you would lead yourself to believe. There is an inherent belief that other people care what you're doing. Aside from family and perhaps a few close friends, they don't care. They have their own lives to run and are buried in their own thoughts and beliefs.

We are often taught that we need to change things on the outside. It's a common sentiment to think that the grass is greener on the other side or that the people around you have more money, or are having a better life than you. It's common to think that others are living a better life on some level. This is simply not the case. If you work on your inside faculties, your life will reach levels you could never imagine. We are conditioned to live through our senses. We can hear, smell, taste and touch. We let the outside world control our minds. We react to what people say or how people respond. We look at our report card and this controls who we believe we are. We look at "not making the team" as who we are. We pay attention to the environment that surrounds us, and often tells us that something can't be done. This turns into messages we tell ourselves and, in turn, informs what our world and life become. The five senses are only good for what they are. It is our reasoning, our intuition and our ability to tell ourselves who we are and how we respond, that creates a fantastic life.

I am not a psychologist, but I know that for some reason the path of least resistance and the easy way are the ways most frequently taken. We all want the best return for the least amount of effort. It's human nature, but it is not possible for most of us, or likely, any of us. The laws of the universe simply don't permit it. The laws of the universe are the same for all of us. What we put in is what we get out. If we want love, we must love. Love doesn't come to people who are haters, those who breathe and speak hate. Money and money retention only comes to people who have a plan and are able to maintain that plan for many years. The Good Book says that you get what you give and this is the absolute truth. Don't question this for a second, as it is one of the universal laws.

Everything you need is inside of you already. You don't need to look any further. You have inside of you what is required to reach your destiny. It just needs to be unlocked. Many of us think that the answer to having our best life lies elsewhere. We think our best life will start when we get that car, that job, find that girl, or make a million dollars.

It's a false bill of goods that we have sold ourselves. Once we become satisfied, at peace, and content in our minds we immediately begin to enjoy our best lives. It will take some work, some perseverance and discipline. In order to understand yourself you will have to learn about the mind and how it works so that you can get in touch with your inner power and strength. My suggestion is to read books, listen to audio tapes and learn from our forefathers.

As much as we think we know it all, we, quite simply, don't. Millions of people have passed before us and it is incumbent on us to learn from these people. The mind is a very powerful organ that controls our destiny. Let's massage it with the most love we can.

CHAPTER 2

WE ALL FAIL - WHO CARES?

If you believe, like I do, that the tough times in life only strengthen you for the future – and many must believe it, since the phrase 'Whatever doesn't kill you can only make you stronger" didn't appear out of thin air – then hop in the DeLorean, because I'd like to take you back a few decades.

I was 25 years old – a recent university graduate with a degree in economics and high-level athletic experience – and after realizing that I had through the years seen nearly every last inch of Vancouver Island, I figured it was as good a time as time as any to spread my proverbial wings and explore other parts of the world – or at least other parts of the province.

So I packed up my life – a few bags and some meagre belongings - boarded a ferry and left for Vancouver, where my girlfriend, who would later become my wife, was already living. I moved in with her immediately, into a small one-bedroom apartment on Davie Street, in the city's west end.

Like many relationships, ours had its ups and downs – made sometimes worse by the fact that we were young and in a city that, for one of us at least, was brand new, unfamiliar, even at times scary. We fought often in those early days – often yelling for hours. Eventually, it became so crazy – so unhealthy for all involved – that I decided it was in the best interests of both of us if I left.

So I did – packing up the same bags and the same meagre possessions I had just a short time before. Only this time, when I stepped out the front door, I didn't have anywhere else to go, nor did I have any money. By chance, I'd recently met a couple of guys my age who were as down on their luck as I was, and one of them happened to have access to the abandoned Lux Theatre in East Vancouver. He'd been a manager at the dilapidated, out-of-business old movie house – located on Hastings Street, in one of the city's more downtrodden neighbourhoods, which even then was notorious for drugs, crime and other undesirable activities.

Five-star accommodations, it was not. But what choice did I have?

So the four of us, with no other options available to us, decided to move into the theatre, which in a previous life had been a brightly-lit neon landmark in a bustling part of the city.

But by that point, brightly lit and full of life it was not. We slept on a few mattresses that were strewn across the floor – clearly, we weren't the first guests to stay there a few days – and we grabbed whatever we could in order to stay warm, as there was no heat and no light. Old, broken furniture was scattered across the room, and the old theatre seats had been torn out of the floor, too. We kept the doors locked at all times, or else we could've easily been robbed, attacked or worse.

We showered at the YMCA, just down the road on Burrard Street, and every morning, we opened our door and look out on all the despair that surrounded us.

I lived there for two weeks, and every day was terrifying. But it wasn't just my surroundings that frightened me – it was also how I felt about myself during those 14 or so days. Forget the college degree, the good suburban upbringing, or my talent on the soccer field, I was just like so many others who were living in my new neighbourhood – a loser who couldn't get his shit together.

It was incredibly sad, how far I'd fallen in that moment, but I never wavered in my belief in myself – not even in those low moments. I always knew I'd make it out of there. Somehow, I'd managed to keep a positive mindset, and was able to view the situation as temporary.

I get my positive outlook on life from my father – a very positive person, and someone who always found the positives in a situation, no matter how bleak it may seem. I always aimed to take after him in that regard, and it's partly because of that philosophy that I didn't tell my parents where I was living. Also, I didn't want to worry them.

In a bit of an ironic twist, today on the site of the old Lux Theatre sits a small apartment development. The old theatre was razed years ago, and the new building was completed in 2009, decades after my friends and I squatted there in squalor, on old mattresses, among the rodents.

Thank God it was only temporary.

* * *

Though those two weeks when I was 25 were among the scariest, shocking and confusing of my life, it wasn't the only time that I, as a young adult, felt like I might stay on the bottom rung of life's ladder forever.

When I was 18-years-old, I applied for a job as a waiter at Dino's Restaurant in my hometown of Victoria. My experience in the restaurant business was, as you might expect of someone that age, limited. At best.

In short – I had no experience whatsoever, aside from having dined there as a customer. At that age, I might not have had the qualifications to even wash dishes, let alone take orders, serve food, clear tables and handle money. So I did what I figured anybody else would do in that situation: I lied. I pumped up my resume, filling it with experience I didn't have, embellishing skills I did not possess, while downplaying any faults.

Of course I got the job.

So there I was on my first day, ready to work but with absolutely no experience whatsoever. Somebody probably had to point me in the direction of the kitchen. But being a confident teenager – and one who possessed that aforementioned positive attitude – I was far less concerned than I should have been. I mean, how hard could it be, right?

In retrospect, my confidence was wildly misplaced.

I still remember serving my first table. With the owner keeping a keen eye on me from a distance, I approached the customers and took their orders – writing them down on my little pad of paper before turning and walking back towards the kitchen. I didn't take their menus away with me – but only because, of course, it never occurred to me that I should.

It took less than a minute for the owner to approach me. Flat out, he asked me again if I actually had any experience as a waiter. Sheepishly, I admitted that I did not.

He asked me to leave, and that was that. I was fired. From start to finish, I'd had the job for less than one hour– my career as a world-class server dashed before my first customers had even finished their complimentary bread.

* * *

I was always a pretty good well-rounded athlete when I was a kid growing up in Victoria, but where I really, truly excelled was on the soccer pitch. I first laced up my cleats when I was in elementary school, and as I grew up and improved, I was lucky enough to have the opportunity to play at the Canandian University level – for my hometown University of Victoria Vikes, no less.

From the first day I pulled that Vikes' jersey over my head in 1988, all I wanted was to win a national championship. It was the goal of every member of our team, of course – why play at that level if you don't intend to win? – but for me, it was all-consuming. We had pretty good teams back then. Some years, we were better than others but we were always competitive, and we always felt like we had a chance when we stepped onto that field.

And though we were a pretty decent team, there was one rather large problem – UBC was good, too. Very good, if the truth be told, and we happened to play in the same conference – Canada West.

Each year, their roster was stacked with high-end talent – players who would go on to play professionally and with Canada's national team. And sometimes, no matter how well you play or how determined or focused you may be, that kind of talent is just tough to overcome. Year in, year out, they'd beat us to advance to nationals. The UBC Thunderbirds had Canada West crowns in 1977, '85 and '86, led by star players like Ian Bridge, who went on to a long professional career in the North American Soccer League while also playing for Canada's national team 34 times – including all three of Canada's World Cup games in 1986.

So yeah, they were good, and in my first four years with the Vikes, they added three more conference titles. In total, they'd go on to win five straight. They dominated nationals, too – winning the title each and every time they'd qualified for the tournament.

Each year we'd try, and each time they'd knock us down.

So when I graduated with a degree in economics, but realized I had one year of soccer eligibility left, I decided to delay my entry into the real world by six months, and I re-registered in school so I could take one last swing at a national championship ring. I desperately wanted to be the very best in Canada, and if that meant I had to spend a semester taking "Intro to Russian" and a few other meaningless classes, well, so be it. Whatever filled the registration requirements was fine by me.

That year, we had a very good team, with what we all thought was a legitimate chance to win. We cruised through the regular season in first place and when playoffs rolled around, it set up like something out of a made-for-TV movie: We had to head to Vancouver to play UBC. The winner went to nationals, the loser went home.

It was raining on game day, and in fact, we dealt with downpours throughout the match. It was ridiculous, how much it rained. But we all dealt with it, and played on. As expected in a game between two rivals, the game was evenly played from start to finish, and was tied at the end of regulation time, and we headed to overtime – two 20-minute periods.

Neither team found the back of the net in the first 20 minutes, but in the second frame, UBC got whistled for a tripping infraction with about 15 minutes left. We were awarded a penalty kick. I always took our team's penalty kicks – it was my specialty. So here I was, with 15 minutes left, ready to win the game for my team.

I approached the ball, and rocketed a shot into the top corner of the net. Destiny. Finally, the mighty Thunderbirds would be vanquished. Finally, I was going to get the chance to play for a national championship.

Or so I thought.

Soccer overtime isn't "sudden death" as it is in some sports, like hockey. UBC still had time to get the equalizer, and with time ticking down, the defending champions did exactly that, tying the game during a goal-mouth scramble with four minutes left to play. We were crushed, but still had a chance – the game was going to penalty kicks.

Each team got five shots, and my coach, Bruce Wilson – knowing full well my talent for such shots – tagged me to shoot first for our team.

I'd taken hundreds of penalty kicks in my life – again, it was kind of my specialty. I liked to pick the corners, and finesse the ball up and into an area of the net that the goalie couldn't possibly reach. I rarely missed. With rain pouring down, I was preparing to make my kick – and give our team an early lead, which would hopefully lead us to victory – when Wilson yells to me three words that entirely changed my approach.

"Just hammer it!" he called out.

Even today, I don't know why he gave me that advice. He knew my game, and knew – or should have known – that my strategy of picking a corner had been successful through the years. But in this instance, he didn't want finesse – he wanted me to kick the ball so hard that it blew clear through the back of the net. In retrospect, I imagine his advice came on the heels of flashback of sorts. Wilson had been a member of that 1986 World Cup team, too, and he'd seen firsthand Bridge famously fire a penalty kick so hard it nearly pulled the netting right off the goal.

None of that helped me in the moment, however. I just stood there in the rain, in the biggest moment of my life, without a clear idea of what to do. Do I place it in the corner like I know I can do? Or do I listen to my coach, and just hammer the ball as hard as I can?

Even as I approached the ball, I didn't know what I would do, but at the last split-second, I took my coach's advice and smashed that ball as hard as I could. The UBC goalkeeper didn't even have to move – the shot hit him right in the shins.

And that was it. We went on to lose the game on penalty kicks, UBC went on to another national title and we went home. For a fifth straight year, I wouldn't get my national championship – I wouldn't even get a chance to compete for one. I was completely gutted, knowing I should have scored that goal. Even now, all these years later, I remember vividly, sitting on the cold tile floor of the shower, head in my hands, water pouring down over me. I felt totally defeated.

All those Russian classes, and for what?

CHAPTER 3

BE CAREFUL WHAT YOU TELL YOURSELF

Being careful of what you tell yourself is, in my opinion, probably one of the most important lessons you can teach yourself. After all, you are the only who has the ability to tell yourself who you, what you have and what you are worth.

How many of you have gone to bed, overcome with negative thoughts – swirling in your head – with regard to some event in your life? You think the same thoughts over and over, pouring over detail after detail, ponder all manner of "what-ifs," and you end up awake for hour, tossing and turning until your alarm rings early the next morning. You can hit the snooze button all you'd like, but it won't change the fact that you wasted hours forecasting negative scenarios that have never happened and possibly never will.

I have done that – we all have at some point in our lives - but I don't anymore, because eventually I realized that those hours constituted time wasted, and time that I will never get back. For sake of argument, let's pretend your hours of restlessness *did* result in you coming up with some good ideas, or a plan to solve whatever problem is stressing you out and causing you to lose sleep. Great – but what are you going to do about it at 3 a.m.?

Your mind twists and turns for hours instead of staying relaxed, being grateful, dreaming up possibilities and conserving your energy for the morning so you can start fresh and with vigor.

I don't know why our minds conjure up all of these negative outcomes, but they do. All of this ruminating is not just a waste of time and energy, but may even serve to create an undesired outcome in the end. There is a simple premise in life that is tested and true – where the mind goes, the energy flows. Whatever you think about will draw on your resources and the laws of the universe. You will attract that which you think most about.

Time is a commodity just like anything else – and perhaps the most important one - so don't waste it. Don't stay up all night with your mind going around in circles. Sometimes you'll fall asleep, only to wake up frightened and disoriented, and your mind will start spinning all over again, like a skipping record.

Instead, tell yourself all the things you are grateful for. Conjure up all the good things about yourself to keep the negative thoughts out. I started to do yoga and meditate 10 minutes a day – barely any time at all! - just so I could learn the art of stopping my negative thoughts. It is my understanding that we have 4,000 thoughts an hour, so let's make sure they are the positive ones. After all, we don't want to let our brains become overwhelmed and suffocated by negativity because once the rabbit hole opens and is not quickly closed, it can lead to real problems that take a long time to solve. So start now by cutting out negative thoughts by whatever method works best for you and your lifestyle. Meditate, do yoga, take long quiet walks in nature, listen to the birds, go for a run, read a book – whatever it takes. For me, the negative thoughts still enter – if we're being honest here, those thoughts can't ever be eliminated 100 percent – but they just don't stay for long. When I first started meditating, I wasn't able to stop the unwanted thoughts. It took weeks of practice until I got to the point where, eventually, I was able to block them from taking up camp in my head. And it was through this process that I devised a motto that has become my new rule of thumb: If it doesn't make me happy, make me laugh, make me money or make me more loving, then I'm not interested. At all. Full stop.

We get to choose what we think. I prefer to spend my time on this earth thinking positively about ideas – big, small and in-between – and other things that truly matter to me. Why would you want to tell yourself things that will make you feel bad? It makes no sense, yet it seems to be human nature. Worrying is, at its root, basically the same as praying for something you don't want to happen.

One of the things I did when I first started to try to control my negative thoughts was to place an elastic band around my wrist - just a small one with some good snap to it. When I had a negative thought or told myself something that wasn't true, I would snap the elastic band on my wrist. It wouldn't hurt, but it would snap be back to where my mind belongs.

It was a gentle reminder – or not-so-gentle, depending on your pain tolerance - that my thoughts should focus on the miracle I am; how much love I have inside of me; how much my family loves me and how fortunate I am to be simply be me. It would snap me back to the reality of how grateful and blessed I am to be on the beautiful ride of life. This is true for all of us. We have been given exactly what we need to reach our destiny and be our true selves. When you tell yourself you aren't pretty enough, athletic enough, big enough, skinny enough - whatever you're telling yourself - you are essentially lying to yourself. It's a way for you to subconsciously justify and accept mediocrity, thus avoiding what you could and should be doing, which is grinding, hustling and finding the "best you."

As humans we love the easy path, the middle ground, the path of least resistance, the known. This way of living is so much easier than getting out of your comfort zone and taking risks. However, that is where the magic in life lies. It lies in the abyss of uncertainty and the uncomfortable. We have all heard a thousand times that it is the man or woman who pushes him or herself to the limit, who fails time and time again yet keeps going, who are revered and honoured in some special way. No matter who we're talking about, I can guarantee you they did not do it for public accolades or recognition. They did it because there was a fire burning inside of them that did not allow them to stop until they were done.

There are hundreds, if not thousands of examples – of both famous and regular people. A 65-year-old woman named

Diana Nyad once swam from Miami to Cuba through the Atlantic Ocean. It took her 45 hours. She didn't sleep, of course, and did not get out of the water. Diana swam with no shark cage. She eventually made it on her sixth attempt. No matter what you may think of a person choosing to attempt such a thing, there is no denying that it is a very impressive feat of human willpower. Do you think she was doing this for recognition or any public accolades? Not a chance. She did this because something inside of her wanted the challenge. She decided that nothing would stop her, and she was doing it for herself so that she could carry on in life as a champion.

Rick Hansen circumnavigated the earth in a wheelchair. Let me repeat that: Rick Hansen circumnavigated planet Earth in a wheelchair. Next time you are near a wheelchair, hop it in and push those wheels quickly for one minute. You will immediately know how difficult this is and you'll be really tired. To have wheeled around the earth – as Hansen did in the mid-1980s on his Man In Motion tour - is the greatest human feat that I have ever witnessed. There was a fire burning inside him that wouldn't be denied, and he stopped at nothing until he achieved his goal. Hansen – who was paralyzed from the waist down in a car accident – embarked on the ambitious challenge not as a way to raise his own profile or gain a level of notoriety for himself, but as a way to raise money and awareness for spinal-cord research.

And, no doubt, he did it because he had something to prove to himself, too. Thirty years later, his Man in Motion tour – and the Rick Hansen Foundation that resulted from it

- continues to provide inspiration and money for its cause. If I ever meet Rick Hansen in person, I will be sure to find out what it was like to tackle this behemoth physical and mental challenge.

Mediocrity, on the flip side, is easy to achieve. In fact, you really don't have to do much to be mediocre. It is essentially, our default position. If you find a job that simply pays your bills, have a spouse or lover that you are not passionate about, have friends who are ambitiously average, or if you watch TV until all hours of the night only to get out of bed in the morning with little passion or excitement, then guess what.... you're well on your way to membership in Club Mediocre.

Life has a way of roughing us all up, making us feel like we are not enough. One of the best-known ways to get ourselves out of this mindset is to be grateful for what we have. This immediately grounds us and brings us into a different vibration. I often think of the love I have in my heart and the love I have for the people in my life. I feel this love daily. I choose to feel grateful for all that has blessed me and for all I have been given: My sight, my family, the work I do, the clothes I wear, the food I eat, and quite simply, the air I breathe.

I encourage you to slow your mind. You don't need anything more or anyone else in order to be grateful. When you show gratitude, you feel good, and this flow of good energy can carry you through the day. Gratitude instantly opens up your mind and allows the multiplication of positive thoughts and feelings. The softening and opening of your heart will give rise to more love and flow. There is a direct correlation. These are often described as vibrations. Have you ever heard the term "good vibe?" Our thoughts influence our vibrations. Our vibrations are what we put out into the world, to the people around us. The mind tells itself how it feels and the body then follows with a vibrational state of being. Be kind to yourself. You just showed up here on earth, and if you're like most of us, you're simply trying your best with no real road map or how-to guide. Most of us have been given a decent upbringing with reasonable teachings from our parents. Many of us, however, haven't been given much direction and guidance. Take it easy on yourself, no matter the background you come from, and don't think yourself to death.

One of the mantras that I use to replace the negative thoughts is from a book called *Zero Limits*, based on the Hawaiian philosophy of Dr. Ihaleakala Hew Len. Basically, Dr. Len's philosophy states that you are responsible for everything that happens in your life. I can hear all the naysayers now: *Well, it's not my fault I got cancer* or *It's not my fault that someone died.* While this may be true in the most literally sense, I suggest looking at this philosophy more in-depth. There is an enormous belief system in humans that suggests someone or something else is responsible for where they are in life, what they have and how they feel. They view how they feel as out of their control. Dr. Len's philosophy says that is not the case. Dr. Len subscribes to the belief that the way to a continuous and prosperous mental environment is to "clean" your own mind first. His mantra is this: *I love you, I am sorry, please forgive me and thank you.* He believes that because we are so hard on ourselves, we need to give ourselves a break and be kinder. It is true that we are so very critical of ourselves. Hence the saying, "We are our own worst enemies."

Dr. Len's mantra softens our heart and mind. It attracts and allows positive people and circumstances into our lives. It calms our busy minds. The mind is a computer and most of the time, we are simply replaying all of the daily negative rubbish that we have seen on TV and have experienced since we were children. Well, guess what? The time has come to end the internal dialogue of the negative mind machine. It is time to change, or stop your negative thoughts and get back on track to being who you really can be. It is time to stop the negative thoughts about your boss, your spouse, your kids, your hair, your lot in life and everything else you tell yourself that is negative. Quit cold turkey – just don't do it anymore. Once the negative thought flow is blocked and replaced with new thoughts, you will be amazed at what opens up to you. The world becomes the magical place you were once told it would be and, really, is supposed to be.

You have everything you need right now and you are perfect the way you are. You just need to change your internal dialogue so you can truly realize not only how great you are in this moment but also how great you can become. Change the internal dialogue, change the things you tell yourself and change your life. Don't spend another moment wasting the energy you have been given. The only way to change how you feel is to change how you think.

One of the ways that I calculate the amount of time that I should spend thinking about something negative is by determining whether or not someone is dying or badly hurt – basically, I catalogue it on a scale of seriousness, with life and death, obviously, being at the top of the chart. If no one's life, safety or general health is at stake, then there is no immediate problem. Therefore, overthinking the situation – whatever it may be - is not likely required. When explaining this to one of my colleagues, the reply I received was, "What about someone who is diagnosed with cancer?" In this case, of course, there definitely is a problem and it requires a plan and discussion. But once the plan is in place and you've figured out the course of action, further negative thought about the cancer would only serve to enhance it.

Where the mind goes, the energy flows.

In this example, laughter, love and happiness in the mind will be the vehicle that will help rid the body of cancer and any disease it may have.

The underlying emotion behind our negative thoughts is fear. We fear the unknown. We fear that we have no idea of the outcome. We become so afraid to do anything because we worry about what might happen, and we can become paralyzed by it.

We know that we need to take risks, think and act differently and rid ourselves of the negative thoughts. True success will only be realized once we get out of our comfort zone and enter the unknown. I have experienced it personally and have read about it even more. We talk ourselves out of the very thing we want the most because we are afraid. Many fears are just excuses to maintain the status quo - self-designed fears to permit us to remain mediocre and not challenge ourselves. When we are afraid of something we avoid it. People who are afraid of heights avoid any activity above ground level, no matter what it is – without considering if such a fear can be overcome, or without wondering if the benefits to said activity outweigh the risks.

I chose the fear-of-heights example specifically, because I know the feeling of being afraid of heights myself. Every time I find myself somewhere high, like on the 30th floor of a building, adrenaline runs through my body. When I look down from a tall bridge my heart jumps into my throat.

Now, this is adrenaline pumping through my body, not fear. There is a difference. True fear would come as a result of life-threatening situations like, for example, being kidnapped by terrorists who are threatening execution with a bag over your head. That is true fear, and something we all hope never to experience.

Having adrenaline course through your body because you are on a Gondola a couple hundred feet above the earth isn't the same – not even close. Though it will often be interpreted as fear, when really you are not afraid of anything. I am sure it happens to anyone who is on a roller coaster or jumping from a plane - being upside-down at travelling 60 km/h on a rollercoaster, or jumping out of a plane from an elevation of 15,000 feet will most certainly create some adrenaline activity. Remember though, this isn't fear. Be careful what you tell yourself and how you categorize your thoughts. People can let fear cripple them.

I was with my father and stepmother recently at our ski-vacation property. I asked my dad if he wanted to go with me up the ski-hill gondola – one of those "open-faced" ones that are not fully enclosed. He wasn't skiing, but I just wanted to go up and down with him. He declined, and told me that he didn't like heights - it made him feel uncomfortable. Fair enough, I suppose. But right then, it occurred to me why I, too, had always told people I was afraid of heights: Because I'd spent my entire life listening to my father saying he was afraid of them.

This idea, naturally, stuck with me and I, too, assumed I was afraid of heights. But no, I am not. Not really. Only I get to tell myself what I am afraid of, who I am and how I live.

The excuse of fear allows oneself to justify the lack of trying and effort. Remember, most of us are comfortable with the easiest path, and having these excuses in our back pockets simply make our life of mediocrity justifiable. Just as it is easy to blame your circumstances on someone and something else, it is as easy to let yourself and your friends know that you're simply afraid. Don't be afraid - have a champion mindset. Challenge your fears and they will no longer be fears. The inertia and the momentum you get from tackling your fears will be enormous and fulfilling, and it will snowball - to your amazement.

You must let go of the fear of the unknown. The unknown is where our best lives live. Our best life is not found inside the mundane activities of life. We need to stretch ourselves because getting outside of our comfort zone is important. See where it takes you. People of substance and achievement have had to stretch themselves outside of their comfort zone in order to find their true love, passion and meaning, and the same is true for all of us.

Sue Whyte, a friend of mine and an equity owner in an investment firm where she had worked for many years, had a good life. She owned two homes, had a steady income, good friends and a great outlook for the future. Yet, she just wasn't satisfied and didn't feel complete. She knew it was time for change. Making a change was a huge step for her – even just the thought of it. She knew that in order to change her future, she first needed to change her daily behaviours and mindset. Sue sold both houses and her portion of her business, at significant profit, and started an internet-marketing company called Snow Angel Marketing. She stepped out of her comfort zone and acted with her heart. Of course she was afraid, but she didn't let this stop her. She took "a leap of faith" in the eyes of many, but in reality, it was actually a leap of action and strategic planning!

She knew, proverbially speaking, that she had to jump off the cliff. She knew that in order to get her life in full order she had some significant decisions to make. She knew her parachute wouldn't open right away and that it would be a bumpy ride down, and that she would likely hit the edge of a cliff or two on the way, but she had faith that her parachute would eventually open. She tested her faith and jumped, selling her partnership equity and leaving her investment business, changing careers, increasing her liquidity and starting over. If you keep repeating the same behaviours, you can expect to get the same results. Don't be afraid of life. It isn't afraid of you.

Fear of the unknown is the primary reason why many people don't end up living life on their terms. They're afraid to lose. Well, guess what, you've already lost if you don't try. It's become something of a tired cliché in the sports world, but the famous quote that has been attributed to hockey legend Wayne Gretzky could not sum up this sentiment any better: "You miss 100 percent of the shots you don't take."

I would rather try and fail than not try at all.

The champion fails more times than the average person tries

— Bruce Lee

Be a champion. Get out there make some mistakes, screw things up and, in the process, learn new ways of doing things. That growth will be the barometer against which you can measure yourself, and tell whether or not you are on the right track. The internal feedback along the way is the guide for your life. What your emotions are, or what you feel, need to be the compass of your life.

Let me tell you a story.

My son is a fantastic soccer player and I have been coaching him since he was five years old. He is now 15 years old, and plays at a high level. One year, a good friend of mine, Chris Walters, and I coached our sons' team all the way to the provincial championship, despite the fact that our team did not have a regular goalkeeper. While it was rare not to have a steady goalie who would play between the pipes day in, day out, we still managed to survive and advance all the way to that big game.

Chris, you see, is a wonderful motivator and is very good at coaching young people. During his own playing days, he played professionally, and he knows the game inside and out, as you'd perhaps expect. At the beginning of the season, knowing that we might have to find success in a somewhat unorthodox manner – again, we were without a net minder – we decided that one of our team's goals would be to get these 13-year-olds into good enough shape so they could out-run opposing players who might wilt in the summer heat. So each day at practice, we would run these kids for long periods of time to increase their stamina and fitness levels.

They would run laps of the field for 20 minutes at a time, often in the heat of the summer. During one of these long runs, I heard the kids start to complain.

"My side hurts," one would say.

"I'm having cramps."

"This is too hard."

They would inevitably slow down or quit running altogether, due to some fabricated complaint in their mind.

Granted, they were young – barely even teenagers – but they were uncomfortable and were searching for excuses that would allow them to stop. I told the kids that of course it's uncomfortable to run for 20 minutes straight in the heat, but instead of complaining, I suggested they tell themselves positive things in order to fend off the negative thoughts.

I tried an experiment. Every time the kids would complain as they ran past where I stood watching them, I would tell them to change their thoughts. I Would advise them to tell themselves they were champions, and that they could do this all day long. I told them to think about how the discomfort would leave shortly, and that it is only temporary. I told them to tell themselves instead that they are fit, can run like deer and that 20 minutes, in the grand scheme of things, is nothing. It would be over before they knew it, I said.

And do you know what happened almost immediately? They stopped complaining, suddenly their cramps went away, their legs didn't feel as tired and they ran like the wind for the entire 20 minutes.

It was a simple shift in thinking that made the run a success.

You see, it is all in what we tell ourselves and what we think about. If we think we are tired, then we'll feel tired; if we think we are lacking, then we are; if we think we are poor, we will be. If we think we can't do something then guess what, we can't. Just as Mahatma Ghandi said, "Men often become what they believe themselves to be. If I believe I cannot do something, it makes me incapable of doing it. But when I believe I can, then I acquire the ability to do it even if I didn't have it in the beginning."

If 13-year-old boys can adjust to this positive train of thought, surely we all can.

Have you ever gone to bed and calculated the amount of time you have to sleep that night? Have you ever lay in bed at 12 o'clock thinking that, because you have to get up at six, you're not going to get your regular eight hours of sleep? Have your thoughts then immediately shifted to how tired you're going to be in the morning? I did this for years. I used to feel fatigued all day if I failed to get the amount of sleep I thought I needed. I reversed my thinking by telling myself that, regardless of the time on the clock, I would wake energized, and more often than not, I did. I would tell myself that I was going to have a fantastic sleep and that I would sleep through the night and get exactly as much sleep as I needed, regardless of what the clock said. I would feel refreshed in the morning and would jump out of bed, ready to tackle the day. It is all in your head. You are what you think.

If you say to yourself each day that you don't like your job, aren't satisfied with your income, your love life, your friends, where you live or how you feel, then I encourage you to take a critical look at your thinking. Don't lie to yourself about your circumstances - be clear on where you are today. Just don't let your circumstances define you and dictate where you go from here. Remember: you get to decide, you are the designer of your life. You get to pick who your friends are, what you listen to, where and who you work with, where you live, what car you drive and any number of other decisions, both big and small. Be courageous and make some changes to your thinking. Things can only improve. What would be the worst possible outcome if you were to make the changes required to live the life you want?

When we ask ourselves this question – "What's the worst than can happen? – we tend to spin into some out-of-control thoughts. What if I'm homeless, have no money, no friends, lose my job, or my significant other leaves me? Blah, blah, blah. Chances are that's not going to happen and you are likely fearing the unknown. You need to change your thought patterns and look at the scenario in a different light.

James Allen writes brilliantly, in his book *As A Man Thinketh,* about the fact that you literally are what you think. He says that you either make or unmake yourself. "By your armory of thoughts you forge the weapons with which you destroy yourself or you fashion the tools with which you build a life of joy, strength and peace."[2]

Allen goes on further to explain that by carefully choosing our thoughts we can reach perfection in life. But if we are abusive with our choices and reckless in our thoughts, we will "descend to the level of a mere animal."[3] Allen believes, as I do, that we are the masters of our thoughts and that through them we can determine our destiny. Allen writes about our minds as analogous to a garden, and suggests that how we tend to it

---

[2] Allen, James, *As A Man Thinketh* (New York: JP Tarcher/Penguin, 2008).
[3] Ibid.

affects its production. He says that by "weeding" out wrong thoughts and "cultivating" right and pure thoughts, you can create outer conditions of your life that are as harmonious as your inner state. Allen reassures us that every stage we are at in life has its purpose, and we are in the perfect positions to learn and grow. He warns against feeling victimized by circumstances and advises that we see ourselves as creative powers in charge of our own development instead. He says it is only when we reach maturity and take responsibility for our condition, that we will progress and discover all of our hidden powers as well as the possibilities that lie within ourselves. According to Allen, thoughts of fear, doubt, indecision, lazy and impure thoughts, hateful and condemnatory thoughts, as well as selfish thoughts lead us to undesirable states. Beautiful, pure, courageous, gentle, loving and forgiving thoughts, on the other hand, will lead us to uplifting and preservative circumstances of peace, freedom, abundance, prosperity and success.

The passage below, also from Allen, confirms everything I have learned since I was 18 years old. It brings clarity to the surface.

"Calmness of mind is one of the beautiful jewels of wisdom. It is the result of long and patient effort in self-control. Its presence is an indication of ripened experience, and of a more than ordinary knowledge of the laws and operations of thought.

A person becomes calm in the measure that one understands themselves as a thought evolved being, for such knowledge necessitates the understanding of others as the result of thought, and as one develops a right understanding, and sees more and more clearly the internal relations of things by the action of cause and effect, one ceases to fuss and fume and worry and grieve, and remains poised, steadfast, serene.

The calm person, having learned how to govern themselves, knows how to adapt themselves to others; and they, in turn, revere their spiritual strength, and feel that they can learn of them and rely upon them. The more tranquil a person becomes, the greater is their success, their influence, their power for good. Even the ordinary trader will find their business prosperity increase as one develops a greater self-control and equanimity, for people will always prefer to deal with a person whose demeanor is strongly equable.

The strong, calm person is always loved and revered. They are like a shade-giving tree in a thirsty land, or a sheltering rock in a storm. Who does not love a tranquil heart, a sweet-tempered, balanced life? It does not matter whether it rains or shines, or what changes come to those possessing these blessings, for they are always sweet, serene, and calm. That exquisite poise of character which we call serenity is the last lesson of culture; it is the flowering of life, the fruitage of the soul. It is precious as wisdom, more to be desired than gold, than even fine gold. How insignificant mere money seeking looks in comparison with a serene life - a life that dwells in the ocean of truth, beneath the waves, beyond the reach of tempests, in the eternal calm!

How many people do we know who sour their lives, who ruin all that is sweet and beautiful by explosive tempers, who destroy their poise of character, and make bad blood? It is a question whether the great majority of people do not ruin their lives and mar their happiness by lack of self-control... few people we meet in life are well-balanced, who have that exquisite poise which is characteristic of the finished character!

Yes, humanity surges with uncontrolled passion, is tumultuous with ungoverned grief, is blown about by anxiety and doubt. Only the wise man - only he whose thoughts are controlled and purified - makes the winds and the storms of the soul obey him.

Tempest-tossed souls, wherever you may be, under whatever conditions you may live, know this: In the ocean of life the isles of blessedness are smiling and the sunny shore of your ideal awaits your coming. Keep your hands firmly upon the helm of thought. In the core of your soul reclines the commanding Master; He does but sleep; wake Him. Self-control is strength. Right thought is mastery. Calmness is power. Say unto your heart, 'Peace. Be still.'"

Flip the negative thoughts into positive ones and tell yourself how your life will look when you execute your new thoughts. Do not stay a slave to what happened yesterday. When you change the way you think, you will change your reality. You can have more satisfaction in your monetary endeavours, you won't have to deal with "those people" at work, you can stretch your creative mind, improve your friendships, and you can have more freedom and more love. If you escape the fear in your mind you can reach the mountaintop. Every person who has stretched their beliefs and let go of fear has found that life is more rewarding and fulfilling. I think we can all agree on this. These people are few and far between.

Some people have lowered their standards and expectations and are happy with where they are in life. If you are one of those people then, please, be happy, it is your right. There also are no right and wrong ways of living. However, if you are like most people, you will have an internal desire for more. You see, as humans we are designed to expand and grow. We are designed to want more, attract more, achieve more, have more, love more, laugh more, give more etc. This is in us at our DNA level. Every successful person I have ever met is always striving for more. Once they get somewhere or reach a goal, they immediately set another.

We must work at life. Life isn't something we were given to just coast through. If you choose to coast, I can assure you will not reap the benefits that life has to offer. Life is meant to be massively fulfilling. We all want these things. The difference is some people will work for them and others won't. Be one of the people who works for life and all it has to offer. When you put in a little bit of effort you will be amazed at the results. You were given the same God-given talents that the person beside you was given. The truth is that some of the people who reach the highest and achieve the most in life are the ones that were given less talent than you. They just worked hard, failed some-times and grew into who they are today. They didn't tell them-selves that they couldn't do it. The man who hiked Kilimanjaro with no legs didn't say, "I can't hike this mountain." The lady who swam from Florida to Cuba didn't tell herself that she couldn't do it. They told themselves it could be done. They weren't sure how many times they would fail, but they told themselves they would do it nonetheless.

When you go to bed at night, remind yourself that you were created as equal to the next person. In fact, you probably have more talent and gifts than the next person, so use them accordingly, don't waste them. Other people would die to have your abilities and talents. The universe loves and rewards people who work hard, fail, get hurt, get back up again to do it all over again until it's done. This is also very personally rewarding and translates into more success down the road. Success breed success. When we win, we feel great and there is usually a natural desire to do it again in order to create the same positive feelings. It is almost like Pavlov's dog, if I could equate it to that. Dopamine is released into the brain when we feel good, so when we win, we keep going back for more.

People with a victim mentality often let failures take them down. I'm sure you know people like this. Friends, family, neighbours and community members you know who feel they have been wronged and are bitter. They believe they can't get ahead because of some set of circumstances that will forever serve as an obstacle.

They key to avoiding this negativity rabbit hole is fairly simple. When you do fail at something, and you will fail at some point, you must not let it set into your psyche or subconscious.

You cannot in any way tell yourself that you are a failure. It is important to remember that you are never a failure when you're attempting to stretch yourself and expand as a human. Your attempt at the event failed, yes. But you are not a failure. There is no one on planet earth who hasn't failed. If you aren't failing enough, then you aren't working hard enough. Get out there and fail. There is no other way to be the best at your endeavour. It doesn't matter whether you play the piano, paint, play soccer, teach, work in a salon or are the Prime Minister: the principles are the same. To be the best, you must work diligently at it for years and years and understand how to fail. Failing is not difficult to accept if you see it as the only way to the top. Once you understand this, striving for the top will become much easier and enjoyable.

Someone asked Thomas Edison (inventor of the light bulb) what it feels like to have failed a thousand times. His response, "I didn't fail a thousand times, it just took a thousand steps to create the light bulb."

Be a little easier on yourself, it will all come in time. We make ideas and concepts in our brains out to be way bigger that they actually are. We take mundane mental circumstances or events and blow them out of proportion.

Once you get started on the task and complete it, it is most often less work and effort than you had originally thought. For example: I cook all of my meals for the week on Sunday. I am not a big cook but I have learned over the years not be caught without food. In order to maintain my ideal weight, I must eat properly. But, in my opinion, there are better things

I could be doing with my time. I would always tell myself, "This is going to take forever," "I don't want to cook today," or "It's Sunday, my day off, and I should be able to relax." My negative campaigning would hijack my brain and suddenly I would start to talk myself out of my task and lead to procrastination. If I actually started cooking I could be finished in about 2 hours, including all the clean-up. I would fool myself into thinking it would take all day when, in fact, it takes only 2 hours. Have you ever done this?

Have you ever allowed a project you didn't want to do to occupy your mind before you even started it, mulling it over and over for days? Often, it's a mundane task that requires little to no thought, but you don't want to do because it would take too much time? Then, when you end up completing the task it turns out it only took half the time you thought it would take? We are our own worst enemies and we make situations and tasks 10 times worse in our minds by thinking negatively. Do yourself a favour and keep your thoughts about these menial tasks positive, and it will save you lots of time and energy

Thinking about yourself as a positive person and focusing on your positive attributes are critical components to how you will feel. How you feel every day is a direct function of what you tell yourself about yourself. I'm not advocating being disillusioned – if you're behaving badly or just generally feeling miserable, you're going to need to take some active steps to get back on track. If you are like most of us, you are an active and contributing member of society, have friends, make good decisions and stay out of trouble. If this is the case, go easy on yourself.

The best part is you get to tell yourself who you are. Tell yourself the right things. Tell yourself that you are a champion, a warrior, one who doesn't quit despite the circumstances. Talk highly of people and don't gossip. Dwell on the positive and not negative events from the past. That is who you "were" and this moment, and all the upcoming future moments is who you "are" and "will be." Don't be defined by your past. So, you made a mistake last week? So what? Don't do it again. Recreate who you are. You can't change your past but you can shape your future. Always remember that it is okay to make a mistake but if you make the same mistake twice, this is no longer a mistake but a decision.

Michael Beckwith, from the movie *The Secret*, seems to put it best. There's a three step approach to letting go of the past and expecting good in the future:

Number one: It is what it is, accept it. It doesn't matter what has happened in your life. Some of you have had disturbing things happen in your past. These things may have really affected your life. Either you are going to control it, or it is going to control you. It is what it is, accept it.

Number two: Harvest the good. Isn't the word "harvest" the best? You can see them bringing in the crops from the field, the fruits of their labour. There is good in everything and the more you look for it, the more you will find. Harvest the good.

Number three: Forgive all the rest. Forgive means to let go of it completely. Abandon. Just let it go. Quit dwelling on what is wrong. Stop thinking about all of the negative things or people in your life. You are blowing these out of proportion. Forgive it all.

It is a very common human condition to dwell on the negative things in life. We dwell on what someone said about us yesterday, the idiot who cut you off in traffic on the commute home (yes, admit it, you're still thinking about it), the person who wronged us, the lack of whatever it is you think you deserve... You get the point - always dwelling on negative things.

Why do negative emotions and negative self-talk in our heads become what often control us? This conditioning certainly starts with our parents and our upbringing. Really look at your parents the next time you see them. Are they excited, are they adventurous, do they have passion about anything in life, how do they speak, what words do they choose, are they negative or positive? This will be your insight, a true look, into the beginnings of who you are. Negative emotions have a bigger impact and lasting impression because we are conditioned to be this way by our environment. Next time you turn on the TV, listen to all the death, rape, destruction, murder and general chaos as you flip from channel to channel. It will startle you once you start really paying attention. The next time the music stops on the radio station you're listening to, and the news comes on, you will hear the same negativity. There are 7.5 billion people in the world. You would be amazed if I told you that .001 percent of the population causes all the world's problems. These few people commit all the murders, the rapes, the explosions, thievery and the chaos. That means that there are almost 7,499,999,999 people doing normal or great things every day. Why are these people so frequently glossed over? We only hear about the very small minority who make poor choices. Here is the completely bizarre part: the actions of this miniscule percentage of the population are what is covered on TV news 95 percent of the time. People like chaos, and the news stations know it.

Remember, TV stations make their money from sponsors who buy time to advertise their products. TV stations examine very closely what gets the highest ratings.

This is just another reason why we place more attention on negativity and chaos. What did I do? I stopped watching the news and turned off the car radio when the news came on. I completely removed myself from all the negative people in my life. I stopped allowing negative people to be around me and speak to me. You can see the energy vampires a mile away, they are easy to spot. You can see it in their eyes, see it in their posture, hear it in their words and feel it in their energy. Do yourself a favour and stay away from these people. Do not give them any of your energy because this is all they want. They need your energy to give life to their energy, regardless of how negative it is. You can't be a negative person if no one is around and there is no one to speak to. They need you to fuel their negativism. Your energy isn't for sale, so don't let them have it. Negative people want to suck you down into their sad abyss. The mental space in your head, as well as your time on earth, is not meant to be given away so cheaply and easily. Reserve the right to say "no" to these people and on your own terms.

So we have two huge reasons, so far, as to why we stay up in bed at night going over the negative thoughts in our minds. We replay all of the negative activities and thoughts of the day. For example: did that person like me? Why did I say it that way? Does she think I'm weird? And on and on it goes.

Bad things have a better chance of happening when you are going over all of the negative thoughts of the day while you should be sleeping. Firstly, you will wake up tired. Secondly, the brain cannot differentiate between what is real and what is not. Let me give you an example. Have you ever had ghost pains or triggers in the brain that cause a certain reaction? Have you ever relived, in your head, the pain of stubbing your toe? Have you ever relived that rejection you received that day? Has your body ever twitched at the thought of something? This is your brain reliving the event and sending the messages to your body, even though the event isn't happening. The brain doesn't know any different. So, the worst part about lying in bed all night with your mind racing is that you are now going through the same negative experience for a second time. You are essentially torturing yourself. Certainly, reflect on the day, considering the feedback you receive can help you shape your character, your words and your life. But don't be a slave to it.

Take some time to reflect on negativity from the day, but spend very little time on it. Recognize it, tell yourself how you will do it differently next time and then let it go. Spend most of your time on the positive - the things you did right, the people you love, the opportunities that are before you and the wonderful moments you had during that day. We have all heard it a million times, but I will say it again in case it isn't burned into your brain: gratitude is the easiest way to bring yourself to the proper state of mind. This is the most important concept. If you are grateful for all that you have in your life, then you cannot help but feel good. If you are stewing about all of the negative things, then you can't help but feel sad and depressed. Being grateful opens a portal for more beautiful things to enter your life. I think we can agree that it is difficult for beautiful and great things to enter your life if you are grumpy, angry, sad and downtrodden. You couldn't see the beautiful and great things if they hit you over the head with a bat. You will be too mired in your negativity and your victim mentality to see the beauty before you. To allow all of the things you want into your life, simply start by being grateful. Be grateful for your life, your eyes, your arms, your breath, your family, and your job (even though you may dislike aspects of it).

Let's cut out the ridiculous sensationalism news, let's turn off the radio, and let's get rid of the negative chatter in our minds. Let's make the words that flow from your mouth pleasant, joyful and positive. I'm not talking about being like Ralph from *Happy Days*, where everything is wildly beautiful and you are as fake as can be. I'm speaking of an authentic ability to genuinely speak both positive and uplifting words. People always ask how you're doing in passing. Instead of saying, "getting by" or "okay" or "same ol'" try "fantastic" or "living the dream." or "I'm having a great day." These words will actually make you feel better. Try it the next time someone asks how you are doing and see how it feels. Part of being peaceful and content is believing that you are actually doing well.

Once you "flip" this around to the positive side you will see your life and the opportunities in it multiply exponentially.

We have been bombarded with media since we were young children. The flow of negativity started in our formative years and it hasn't stopped, only ramped up. It is enormous. It starts in the morning and doesn't stop all day. It is everywhere. And with the onset of social media, the flow of negativity is absolutely relentless. Every day, all day we are hammered with the same message. Death is everywhere, destruction is rampant, the economy is no good, and struggle is the way of life…blah, blah, blah.

But no, it isn't actually that way. Ask the people around you who are successful and happy. They will tell you a different story. They will tell you stories of abundance, happiness, joy, adventure and being fulfilled.

I want to end this chapter with these words on the Affirmative Power from Thomas Troward:

"To realize the true nature of affirmative power is to possess the key to the great secret. We feel its presence in all the innumerable forms of life by which we are surrounded and we feel it as the life in ourselves; and at last someday the truth bursts upon us like a revelation that we can wield this power, this life, by the process of Thought. And as soon as we see this, the importance of regulating our thinking begins to dawn upon us. We ask ourselves what this thought process is, and we then find that it is thinking affirmative force into forms which are the product of our own thought. We mentally conceive the form and then think life into it.

This must always be the nature of the creative process on whatever scale, whether on the grand scale of the Universal Cosmic Mind or on the miniature scale of the individual mind; the difference is only in degree and not in kind. We may picture the mental machinery by which this is done in the way that best satisfies our intellect—and the satisfying of the intellect on this point is a potent factor in giving us that confidence in our mental action without which we can affect nothing—but the actual externalisation is the result of something more powerful than a merely intellectual apprehension. It is the result of that inner mental state which, for want of a better word, we may call our emotional conception of ourselves. It is the "self" which we *feel* ourselves to be which takes forms of our own creating. For this reason, our thought must be so grounded upon knowledge that we shall feel the truth of it, and thus be able to produce in ourselves that mental attitude of feeling which corresponds to the condition which we desire to externalise.

We cannot think into manifestation a different sort of life to that which we realize in ourselves. As Horace says, *"Nemo dat quod non habet,"* we cannot give what we have not got. And, on the other hand, we can never cease creating forms of some sort by our mental activity, thinking life into them. This point must be very carefully noted. We cannot sit still producing nothing: the mental machinery *will* keep on turning out work of some sort, and it rests with us to determine of what sort it shall be. In our entire ignorance or imperfect realisation of this we create negative forms and think life into them. We create forms of death, sickness, sorrow, trouble, and limitation of all sorts, and then think life into these forms; with the result that, however non-existent in themselves, to us they become realities and throw their shadow across the path which would otherwise be bright with the many-coloured beauties of innumerable flowers and the glory of the sunshine.

This need not be. It is giving to the negative an affirmative force which does not belong to it. Consider what is meant by the negative. It is the absence of something. It is not-being, and is the absence of all that constitutes being. Left to itself, it remains in its own nothingness, and it only assumes form and activity when we give these to it by our thought.

Here, then, is the great reason for practising control over our thought. It is the one and only instrument we have to work with, but it is an instrument which works with the greatest certainty, for limitation if we think limitation, for enlargement if we think enlargement. Our thought as feeling is the magnet which draws to us those conditions which accurately correspond to itself. This is the meaning of the saying that "thoughts are things." But, you say, how can I think differently from the circumstances? Certainly you are not required to say that the circumstances *at the present moment* are what they are not; to say so would be untrue; but what is wanted is not to think from the standpoint of circumstances at all. Think from that interior standpoint where there are no circumstances, and from whence you can dictate what circumstances shall be, and then leave the circumstances to take care of themselves.

Do not think of this, that, or the other particular *circumstances* of health, peace, etc., but of health, peace, and prosperity themselves. Here is an advertisement from *Pearson's Weekly*: "Think money. Big money-makers *think* money." This is a perfectly sound statement of the power of thought, although it is only an advertisement; but we may make an advance beyond thinking "money." We can think "Life" in all its fullness, together with that perfect harmony of conditions which includes all that we need of money and a thousand other good things besides, for some of which money stands as the symbol of exchangeable value, while others cannot be estimated by so material a standard.

Therefore, think life, illumination, harmony, prosperity, happiness—think the things rather than this or that condition of them. And then by the sure operation of the Universal Law these things will form themselves into the shapes best suited to your particular case, and will enter your life as active, living forces, which will never depart from you because you know them to be part and parcel of your own being.[4]"

---

[4] Troward, T. (1921). *The hidden power: And other papers on mental science.* New York: Dodd, Mead.

CHAPTER 4

SUCCESS AND FAILURE

I wish that I'd known at a much younger age just how much I would fail in life. Knowing that many successful people have failed – and failed often - would have definitely given me a different perspective on failure. Had I realized this back then, I would have seen failure as not only necessary, but as a stepping stone to eventual achievement. In order to achieve, you will likely fail before you get there. It often takes years of struggling to reach the top of your mountain.

"The man on top of the mountain didn't fall there."

— Vince Lombardi

This fact is indisputable. No one has ever gotten to the top of the mountain without falling down, failing miserably, having to start over and getting their ego knocked around. The examples of people failing over and over again until they succeed are endless. Not everyone who's on top today got there with success after success. Here are 10 great examples of people throughout time that have worked hard, struggled, and failed repeatedly:

1. **Henry Ford:** While Ford is today known for his innovative assembly line and American-made cars – and for a brand that has become, in many ways, synonymous with America - he wasn't an instant success. In fact, a number of his early businesses failed and left him broke and penniless five times before he founded the successful Ford Motor Company.

2. **R. H. Macy:** Most people are familiar with the large department store chain that bears his last name, but Macy didn't always have it easy. Macy started seven failed businesses before finally hitting big with his first Macy's store in New York City.

3. **F. W. Woolworth:** Some may not know this name today, but Woolworth was once one of the biggest names the U.S. department store game. Before starting his own business, young Woolworth worked at a dry goods store, but was not allowed to wait on customers because his boss said he lacked the sense needed to do so.

4. **Oshiro Honda:** The billion-dollar business that is Honda began with a series of failures and fortunate turns of luck. Honda was turned down by Toyota Motor Corporation for a job there after interviewing for a job as an engineer, leaving him jobless for quite some time. He started making scooters of his own at home, and

spurred on by his neighbours, finally started his own business. I'd say it all worked out for him.

5. **Akio Morita:** You may not have heard of Morita, but you've undoubtedly heard of his company, Sony. Sony's first product was a rice cooker that unfortunately didn't cook rice so much as burn it, selling less than 100 units. This first setback didn't stop Morita and his partners as they pushed forward to create a multi-billion-dollar company that is among the world's largest today.

6. **Bill Gates:** Gates didn't seem like a shoe-in for success after dropping out of Harvard and starting a business with Microsoft co-founder Paul Allen called Traf-O-Data which failed. While this early idea didn't work, Gates' later work did, creating the global empire that is Microsoft. The computer magnate is among the world's richest people, as well as one of the most generous philanthropists.

7. **Harland David Sanders:** Perhaps better known as Colonel Sanders of Kentucky Fried Chicken fame, Sanders had a hard time selling his chicken at first. In fact, his famous secret chicken recipe was rejected 1,009 times before a restaurant finally accepted it. Now, that same recipe is protected under lock and key.

8. **Walt Disney:** Today, Disney rakes in billions from merchandise, movies and theme parks around the world, but Walt Disney himself had a bit of a rough start. He was fired by a newspaper editor because, as he was told, he lacked imagination and had no good ideas. After that, Disney started a number of

businesses that didn't last long and which ended in bankruptcy and failure. He kept plugging along, however, and eventually found a recipe for success that worked.

9. **Thomas Edison:** In his early years, teachers told Edison he was "too stupid to learn anything." Work was no better, as he was fired from his first two jobs for not being productive enough. Even as an inventor, Edison made 1,000 unsuccessful attempts at inventing the light bulb. Of course, all those unsuccessful attempts finally resulted in the design that worked.

10. **Orville and Wilbur Wright:** These brothers battled depression and family illness before starting the bicycle shop that would lead them to experimenting with flight. After numerous attempts at creating flying machines, several years of hard work and tons of failed prototypes later, the brothers finally created a plane that could get airborne and stay there.

This list goes on and on. There are millions of people who have been hugely successful. These people were successful primarily because they had passion and drive in their purpose that kept them going.

The irony of the road to success being rife with pitfalls is that long before you ever hit the jackpot, you're already successful if you have committed to betterment, growth and abundance. Before you embark on any journey, recognise that you've got the tools within you to succeed, the capacity to learn a tremendous amount, and the ability to develop an invincible mindset. Once you have committed yourself 100 percent to your goal, that's the point at which you will become success-ful. It's been taught to us from the very beginning that it is at the end of the journey where we receive the prize, or achieve success. This is wrong, wrong, wrong. We have all heard a thousand times that it is the journey and not the destination, to enjoy the moment, to be present and to be sure not to get a head of yourself. Do yourself a favour and burn these con-cepts into your being - they are a big deal and will be most helpful in your journey.

The problem with not enjoying the journey and letting the end result be the measuring stick by which you mark success is that the end is often far less satisfying that we expected it to be. It also doesn't last long. You know what I'm saying - reaching a goal only feels good for a brief time, maybe an hour, maybe a day, maybe a week. Then the feeling wears off and it's on to the next challenge. Meanwhile, you toiled for years to get there. Do you see that this is disproportionate? It should be reversed; you should toil for a day or a week to reach that goal that satisfies you for a long time. We all know that this is not the case, however, and that life isn't this way. We all know by now that in order to reach a goal, we need to work diligently for a long time.

This is why it is so important to enjoy the journey and recog-nize that you are successful once you have committed your-self to the challenge. Every day that you work towards that goal will feel like a successful one if you believe in your suc-cess and can see yourself moving in the right direction. The lingering doubts and fears will disappear once you commit to the task and enjoy the journey, and all the ups and downs, wins and losses. Your mind will become free of all its mental clutter. This is when life starts to feel easy and flow like water down a river.

Sometimes everything you seek is right where you started. This will become clearer once you drop the mental veil that consumes you daily. With a loving and open heart, you will be on the path to living your fullest and most enjoyable life. Often along our journey to success and fulfillment, we realize that everything we wanted and needed is right where we started. We are often seeking something external to make us happy or fulfill us – a new job, a shiny new car, a new watch, a summer home maybe. This search manifests itself as a search for money, fame and success. The search is not necessary, however, because we already have everything we need inside of us, and by virtue of this we shall all get what we want.

When I was young and I failed, I would take it personally. My inner thoughts were exactly what'd you'd expect: that I wasn't good enough, smart enough, talented enough, didn't work hard enough or just didn't have what it took to win. What a mistake that was. If I had simply realized that failures are the necessary stepping stones to something better, I would have viewed these failures completely differently. My internal dialogue would have been different. It would have said something like, "I am that much closer to success because I failed again. No one gets it on their first, second or third try." I would have told myself that this failure has nothing to do with my abilities, it just means I need to keep going a little bit longer and push forward a little bit more. If I want something badly enough, I have to keep going until I get it.

You see, success doesn't care what you look like, what your weight is, what your gender is or how high your IQ is. Success only rewards the people who are prepared to get knocked down, get back up and keep going. In the cases above, it is difficult to imagine how many times they failed and got back up. Truly remarkable stuff.

Many of us were taught growing up that you have to get "it" whatever "it" is… to become whatever you want to be. You don't have to *get* anything. You've got it. I didn't *get* anything to go from being broke and living in a condemned theatre to having the kind of life I have now. I just became aware of what I already had.

We need to fail in order to truly achieve what we are destined to achieve. It cannot be avoided. You may have heard of, or know people who grew up with, the proverbial silver spoon. These are the people who seemed to have it better than us right from the start. Maybe they grew up with wealthy parents, or received a large inheritance at a young age, or were groomed to take over the successful family business from the time they graduated high school.

How does this story translate in your head? Let me guess: they didn't have to work hard to get what they have. They are different, you say to yourself. They are lucky, they've got it easy. These are typically the things we think about successful people. What we don't see are the years of discipline, struggle, repetition and hard work that preceded their success – whether it was their own personal struggle or that of their family. Working hard and failing, forges character and provides you with the life skills to keep you on top. I'm not saying that all people who have been given a "leg up" don't stay on top. While there are stories upon stories of the successful person falling from grace, if they have had the benefit of a solid upbringing they are, more often that not, fine. My point is that it is difficult to teach others, including your children, the pain and importance of failure. For some reason as humans we need to experience first-hand the pain of failure and joy of success to truly appreciate them and learn from them.

"There is a world operating within you. A wonderful world. We want to try to understand that. Your spiritual DNA is perfect. It requires no modification, no improvement. There is absolute perfection within you. It is really important that we get this. It doesn't have to be modified, it doesn't have to be changed. All you have to do is let it come to the surface. When you stretch and go for something you really love that is beyond what you think you can do, you will find that you can perform much better than you imagined. You become aware that there is the ability within that you previously failed to recognize."

— Bob Proctor

When you don't make the team, when you fail an exam, when you get told you're not good enough, when you feel weak and your internal dialogue is negative, remember these things:

1. If you want success badly enough you CAN get it by continuing to pursue the goal and realizing that the failures are a necessary step.
2. No one really cares about your successes and failures as much as you think they do. You must care massively.

"You may encounter many defeats, but you must not be defeated. In fact, it may be necessary to encounter the defeats, so you can know who you are, what you can rise from, how you can still come out of it."

— *Maya Angelou*

I am sure your parents will care about your failures and successes. Your close friends and other family members, too. But I'm also certain that the rest of the people around you really don't care - they are too busy worrying about themselves. We seem to think that people think about us at a disproportionate level. I want to blow this idea right out of the water and out of your head. Stop spending so much time consumed with what others think about you. They are not thinking of you and you are wasting your time. That may be tough to swallow, but it's usually true.

I would like to use an example from when I was growing up. I was a sports enthusiast, playing two sports a season.

At university, I continued to play varsity soccer and some semi-professional soccer. During these times I was in the gym a lot, lifting weights. When I surveyed the gym environment I would see guys lifting heavy weights. My ego would lead me to believe that these people were actually looking at me and calculating how much weight I was lifting. My belief was that they would then judge me based on how much I could lift. Anyone who has gone to the gym has probably experienced this feeling. Talk about crazy internal dialogue. As these immature beliefs manifested, I increased the possibility of injuring myself. As I aged and my ego shrunk, I realized that literally nobody was watching me. No one gave a rat's ass about how much weight I was lifting or if I was even lifting anything at all. I wasted so much time thinking about what other people thought when in reality, none of it mattered. It was wasted energy.

Imagine the time I would have saved had I just realized this at the time. Imagine the difference it would have made if I had just saved all the mental anguish that came with worrying about what other people thought. Just imagine the gains I would have enjoyed if I simply stayed focused on *my* plan and *my* goals and didn't worry about anything else. The amount of time you can save if when you drop the veil of your self-importance is incredible. You're one person in 7.5 billion people. I am not trying to be negative, but the facts are the facts, get over yourself. Once you are able to accomplish this, you will make fantastic gains and strides in your life. You will save so much mental energy by not worrying about nonsense. Once you get into a position in life where you are impacting and helping other people, *then* you will start to be noticed. People will truly start to care about you. And for the right reasons, to boot.

We have an internal, overinflated importance about ourselves, which is probably a good thing in the long run. This self- importance serves as a survival mechanism, which is healthy. If we all thought we were losers, then what would be the point of going on? Just be careful of having an overzealous ego where you think everyone cares about your life and your failures and successes. Everyone is trying to achieve the same things that you and I are trying to achieve in life.

Nothing will stop some people from desiring success. Let me be clear about what success means to me. When I was younger, I was taught, and as a result internalized, that success was only defined by finances. I had to get something in order to be successful - something tangible like a car or a house or a bigger savings account. My definition of success has changed through my life's experiences, however. Balance, of all the things we want and strive for in life, is now my definition of success. Love, happiness, money, peace of mind, health, some security, spirituality and the ability to contribute to society are paramount. To varying degrees, it is safe to say that we all want the following things in our lives:

1. Love
2. Strong family connections
3. Spirituality
4. Security or money

5. A good job
6. Good friends
7. Travel
8. Good health
9. Leisure time

I began to realize that there is more to success than money, and it is the amalgamation of the above that truly creates success for me. You've all heard of the man who has a lot of money and isn't happy. That's because he has voids in the other areas of his life. Having money will only serve to magnify your current feelings. If you have a good attitude and are happy before you have money, this will continue. If you are sad, angry or discontent before you have money, you will only get more of this. You see, money is the great magnifier, it often shines a bright light on who you already are.

Maybe the rich man is lonely because he spends all his time making money and forgot about love. Maybe he or she is overweight because they spend all their time focused on earning money and don't make it to the gym. Don't just settle for one or the other. Try to get them all. Once you have balance, the universe tells us and shows us regularly that whatever you are attracting or wanting more of will flow to you. If you are out of sync and out of balance, your results will show it. In other words, you must be filled with positive thoughts, with negative thoughts nowhere in your subconscious. It is in this state where the laws of attraction unveil themselves. It is in this state when the world and the people in it start to line up.

Your own mission is the most important aspect of your life. Everyone needs a purpose, this is what gives you drive and ambition. When you know your purpose, you can be more dedicated to building your skills. Your motivation improves as does your clarity for the future.

Your relationships with family, friends and yourself will improve dramatically because you're living authentically with your real purpose in mind. You're fulfilling it – or moving in that direction – every, single day. Your finances improve because you are adding massive value to your life. Your free time expands because you've created your ideal life based on your passions. Hopefully you can recognize how clarifying your purpose in life can make everything else easier.

Also, it adds value to your love life, because you heart is open. There is an anecdote in the story *The Alchemist* in which the main character Santiago is faced with a choice between his love, Fatima, or his mission. He goes to the fortune teller who tells him he could choose her first, and he would be happy, for a time. After these short years, havoc would wreak itself on the village he led because he did not give the world his gift. In the end, he chose to leave her and pursue his mission, and was able to regain her love and relationship after he fulfilled his mission.

It's like this for us, too. If you're not willing to throw it all away for the greater good – to take some risks - it's not going to end well.

Whoever said, "life is short" was mistaken. Life is the longest journey you'll ever go through. Only one reality is longer than life: death. Until you face death, anything you deal with is temporary. The saying should be: "Life is long, setbacks are short."

However, setbacks are a part of life. It is often through these setbacks that life teaches us lessons. Most of us are too hard-headed to learn a real lesson without them. Many people allow setbacks to set them back further, as it's easy to regard a demotion to a lower rung as permanent. Once you reframe your conscious to believe setbacks are short, and life is long, you will start to look at problems and struggles differently. Facing adversity, knowing it is temporary, makes our trials much easier to endure. Having the mindset of "I'll get through this, it is only temporary," is a game changer. It is the mindset of the mentally tough.

When you lose, it feels like you're a loser and you often hear someone called as such. When you hear that enough times it can start to sink into your psyche. So here's the deal: you may have "lost" at that single effort or attempt, but you are not a "loser". If you hear this word being used in reference to yourself or someone else just remember that you will make mistakes and there will be obstacles in your way. Pay no attention to the naysayers. If you want something badly enough and you're passionate enough about it, then nothing can stop you. You can handle obstacles and setbacks like a champion and a winner.

Once you have retrained your thoughts, the next step is to get over the hurdle as quickly as possible. I've found the best way to surpass a setback is to do what I call "the arrow." An arrow is pulled back until it reaches the optimum amount of stress and tension on the cable. At some point, a "trigger" is pulled and the cable releases, launching a weapon at full speed. Even though the arrow is only stretched back a few feet, the momentum springs the weapon forward with tremendous distance – and at high velocity.

Picture yourself as that catapult. You hit stress and tension, which pulls you back - just short of your limit. Then, after a brief period of time, some sort of trigger in your life causes you to use that tension and stress to spring you ahead with powerful force.

When you face hard times, look for the "trigger" to release you from your tension and stress, the setting will launch you into momentum. Instead of feeling down and out about the turn of events, shift your focus to finding the trigger. As soon as you see yourself hitting a setback, start looking for it and realize this is not a setback but a set up to catapult you to where you need to be in life.

Once you find it, the next step is to pull it! Use it to shoot you skyward to new heights that you thought were previously out of reach. Use it to gather steam to launch onward. And don't stop until you have hit the ground. Then when you do, take off running. Use every bit of momentum available.

You now know that setbacks are the pivot point for momentum. Having this mindset allows you to actually look forward to setbacks and failures that befall everyone. After all, if you believe what I am sharing with you, that setbacks or failure are essential to attaining massive gains in your life, then you can recognize setbacks as good things and can welcome them on the path to your success.

Bottom line: next time you're experiencing a setback or failure, think of it in a positive light. It's a good thing and it's also just a stopgap in your long life. The faster you can find the trigger and get back on top of your game, the faster you'll hit your highest point.

There is a reason why "the cream rises to the top," and that an estimated three percent of the world control 97 percent of all the money. It is because these people understood this principle and never allowed the naysayers to dissuade them. When winners lose, they know they are one step closer to their goal of winning. They see it differently than the others do. Losing motivates winners to win even more. So go ahead and lose. Lose often because at least that means you're on the right track to wherever your destiny lies. Be a winner, be a champion. It is in you already, waiting to reveal itself.

CHAPTER 5

THE MYTH OF UNIVERSITY

God bless my parents, they tried their best and gave 100 percent effort raising their family. They were successful; my brother, my sister and I grew up as regular kids and had all the things that we needed and most of what we wanted. We grew up in Victoria on the west coast of Canada. I had a fairly textbook upbringing, did well in sports, got good grades and moved on to university. My parents taught us everything they knew.

But there was just one problem: they, like everyone else, only knew so much. They weren't given a road map to life when they were kids, and when they grew up all they could do was pass down to us what they knew. They knew what their parents taught them, and the cycle continues.

As an example, a lot of people smoked cigarettes back in the day. I woke every morning greeted by thick clouds of smoke in the kitchen where I ate breakfast. As I rose from bed, brushed my teeth and went upstairs to be with my family for breakfast, my mom and dad would already be three or four cigarettes into their day. Entering the kitchen would be like entering a wall of smoke. I asked my dad later on in life, what that was all about, his reply was, "We didn't know any better back then." In his defence it wasn't until decades later that we truly begin to understand about multitude of toxic chemicals found in cigarettes.

My point is that they didn't know any better, and they couldn't teach us what they didn't know. Let's not kid ourselves, our parents came from a slightly different era. They loved us unconditionally, of course, and gave us whatever they could. However, they weren't able to provide us with information that could have lead us to live much easier and better quality lives.

My parents said, "You have to go to university, son." This was the message that I heard over and over for years, from the time I was very young.

I never questioned it, either, as my gut feeling was that it sounded like a sensible thing to do. I would go to university. My parents, society, and my own instincts, told me that if I educated myself I would be able to get a better job.

Me: Why do I have to go to university, what is in it for me?

Dad: Well, son, you learn more and you become educated and then employers will hire you because you have a degree. It's just what people do.

With a good job I would earn money, buy a house, have a family and live happily ever after.

Wow, was I in for a bumpy ride.

Straight out of high school, where I was awarded male athlete of the year, I accepted a soccer scholarship and went to the

University of Victoria. I was on the right track - according to society and my parents, everyone was winning. I showed up on the first day of university and I was asked which classes I wanted to take. I didn't know. The man said that he couldn't help me choose my degree. My next thoughts were centered around trying to figure out what I liked and what makes me happy.

"Children," was my immediate thought. I like being around children, teaching them and inspiring them to be the best they can be. So I signed up for a teaching degree.

"I'll be a teacher" I said to myself, right there on the spot, as I enrolled with no insight, research, passion or plan.

I took education classes for the first year of university but then decided I didn't want to be a teacher. My gut feeling was that business was a possibility. My brother, Eric, was studying economics so I thought that I might enjoy it as well. Fast forward five years, I had completed my degree in economics and played five years of varsity soccer. I felt that these were big accomplishments and I revelled in the success. This was until it was time to get a job and make money, like my parents and society told me would happen next. After getting a degree in economics I thought employers would be banging down my door offering me huge opportunities to make money. I mean, why wouldn't they? I am Bruce Ellemo, of course. At 26, I had an inflated belief about the importance of my economics degree, I thought I was unstoppable and well on my way to riches. There wasn't anything further from the truth.

After university, I worked at the local Canadian Tire making $5.75 per hour. I also had a stint working at a movie store, which was popular back in the day. Nobody who paid well wanted to hire a guy with a general degree in economics. I felt like I'd been tricked. Why in the world would I spend five years studying and incur $32,000 in student loans, only so I could earn $5.75 per hour? Where was the payoff? Where was the bucket of gold at the end of the rainbow? There wasn't one. I was sold a false bill of goods.

My education taught me almost nothing about what an employer would want. All I knew was how to regurgitate information. I knew some supply and demand functions and some other clever economics equations, but I had no real life skills or work experience. Would anyone hire me just because I knew the future value of a cash flow series? Not likely.

In 1992, while I was working at Canadian Tire, I had to live in a basement suite with a friend. Rent was $400 per month. The suite was dark and had very little natural light. The homeowners lived upstairs. I drove an old Volkswagen Rabbit that I bought for $2,000. I had the essential basics of life – job, vehicle and a roof over my head.

To put this in comparison, let me tell you a story of a person I befriended later in life. This person had a completely different way of thinking than me. He decided well before he started high school what he intended to be, and had chosen his future profession much earlier than I did. As you recall, I walked into university on the first day and didn't know which classes I wanted to take. My friend had known the whole time. He wanted to be a doctor. There are hundreds of professions, of course - you don't need to want to be a doctor, you just need to want to be something.

When you have created a path or have an understanding of where you want to go it is much easier to get there. Without any idea at all, you will most certainly flounder, as I did. During my friend's last years of high school, he chose the courses that would get him on the path to being a doctor. He did four years of undergraduate work, then immediately stepped into the three years of post-graduate work, followed by one year as an intern doctor. This is the path he needed to follow in order to be a doctor, and he did it.

Let's take a look at the differences of knowing your goal and not knowing your goal. My friend graduated as a doctor at 26 years old. Immediately out of school he began to earn $300,000 per year at his own walk-in clinic. Within five years he was one of the highest paid doctors in British Columbia earning $800,000 per year. He drove fancy cars and lived in beautiful homes.

Then there was me – same age, with a degree from the same school. I was driving a $2,000 car, living in a dingy basement suite and earning darn near minimum wage while working for someone else. I was also $32,000 in debt. The big point here is that if you are going to go to school and spend your time and money then at the very least know what the outcome will be before you get started. Don't go in blind just because your parents and society told you to go to school.

Being an English major isn't going to do much for your standard of living when you graduate if you don't plan on using that degree to become a teacher or something similar. A degree in history will not often pay your bills. These are noble subjects and endeavours, but if you are pursuing these majors, you should consider further education that specializes in your area. You will need at least an MBA or doctorate-level degree in order to make it worth your while.

There are three options that we must choose.

Option #1

Don't go to high school and university at all - the history of the world is riddled with people who didn't go to university and went on to be extremely successful. Here are some examples:

- Mark Zuckerberg left Harvard to invent that site you spend way too much time on.
- Media mogul Russell Simmons dropped out of Manhattan City College just shy of finishing his sociology degree.
- Brad Pitt was set to be a journalist when he dropped out of the University of Missouri two weeks before graduation.
- Ted Turner, the creator CNN and the 24-hour news cycle, was expelled from Brown University after he was caught with a girl in his room. GASP!
- Steve Jobs dropped out of Reed College to become the father of all things Apple.

- Oprah Winfrey dropped out of Tennessee State University and seems to be doing all right.
- Bill Gates dropped out of Harvard to pursue his love of poetry. Just kidding, he founded Microsoft.
- Before YOLO, there was POLO. Ralph Lauren left Baruch College after two semesters to serve in the U.S. Army, and the rest, as they say, is history.
- John Lennon was expelled from Liverpool College, so he joined a band. Maybe you've heard of them.
- Jim Carrey dropped out of high school at 16. "Alrighty then!"
- After failing every subject except English, Al Pacino dropped out of his New York high school to pursue acting.
- Wolfgang Puck quit school at the ripe young age of 14 to become a cooking apprentice at a hotel.
- Walt Disney dropped out of high school at 16, joined the Red Cross, and left for Europe.

The list goes on and on.

Life's lessons can be the most valuable. Practical experience at a job is often just as valuable, if not more so, than formal education. The problem with formal education, at least at the undergraduate level, is that it is too general and has limited practical application in the work place. Who wants to hire a person because he or she knows when Napoleon conquered Egypt or King Kamehameha conquered Hawaii? The answer is no one. Employers want people who can make them money.

In today's world, you can create and become who you want at an early age. The most important thing, if you don't go to school, is to find a passion for something and let it drive you to success. Find what you love to do and do it often. If you go out into the world with no formal education and no passion for making money, you will be swallowed up. This has happened to millions of people. We all know people who go to their jobs just because they have to pay the bills. This is not how you want to go through life, " just paying the bills".

If you enter your adult life without some kind of a passion, or at least a working life plan, the chances are you will get sucked into the vortex of mediocrity. I was there. I know what it is like and frankly, it sucks compared to the alternative. The alternative is filled with purpose, fulfillment and in a lot of cases very good income. The people who make the most money or are the most successful are extremely passionate about what they do. They would more than likely be considered experts based on the amount of time they have spent following their passion.

Option #2

Go to university – but go with a plan that starts in high school. Know what you want and make a plan to get there. Once out of high school, you can enter the next level – university - knowing exactly the courses you will need to take over the next four years. From there you can enter post-graduate education on course and on target. Once that is over, you have become more specialized than the average degree holder which will serve you better in the work force. To become even more specialized, go on to some doctorate work and get your PhD. From there you will be off and running at 25-28 years old.

Option #3

Get yourself a trade. As long as the earth is here and there are people on it, we will need tradespeople. The trades include electricians, pipe fitters, welders, accountants, stonemasons, carpenters, butchers, etc. These trades are the heart and soul of our country and make up a larger percentage of all employment. Be an apprentice, get your ticket and work for someone else while you get your feet on the ground and establish some cash flow and bank some money. If you become really passionate about the business you are in, then I recommend squirrelling away a bit of cash and use it to start your own business. There will be some risk and as always, it will take some courage. Forge on and jump off the cliff, take a risk – more often than not, the parachute will open. It has to start somewhere. The people who own the large successful construction companies all started at the same place, right here. It's like my dear friend, extremely successful entrepreneur and mentor, Mr. David Nickel always says, "Someone owns Visa."

It doesn't matter which route you take, what matters is that you pick one and have a plan. Don't just flounder through life and see what happens. You must decide what you want and how you want to live. Then go out and get it. The universe owes you nothing. The reverse is true: you owe the universe. Go out and make your mark, be the best damn carpenter the planet has ever seen. Be the best chef that you can possibly be. When we become highly skilled, the universe stands up and takes notice. It opens up doors and opportunities that you would never have imagined. When you combine this professionalism with hard work and perseverance, that's when you can achieve greatness.

The rule or lesson I learned through all of this can be summed up in the following quote.

"There are two paths people can take. They can either play now and pay later, or pay now and play later. Regardless of the choice, one thing is certain. Life will demand a payment."

— John Maxwell

Translated, this means you can take the route of my friend who was a doctor by 26 years old and making $300,000 per year or you can float though life with no idea like me - live in a basement suite after university graduation, working at Canadian Tire. Your call. You make the choice – it's your life, you get to design it. Neither is right, neither is wrong.

However, in hindsight, I can tell you that of the two choices, I would imagine one is more enjoyable than the other.

Once you have developed a plan it will be much easier to execute it. If you are like most people you may only have a general idea about what you want in life. That's OK.

You may only have a general idea of how you want to live, how much cash flow will be required and what exactly you want to be doing. Make a plan early on in the process and it will benefit you greatly in the long run. We all have friends who have done this successfully and we all have friends who haven't. The contrast between the people who have had a plan and those who didn't is amazing.

Those who created a plan and followed it are often the ones who are deemed to be successful in terms of wealth and quality of employment. It is the people who have no plan that seem to be the ones who are working in jobs they don't like just to pay the bills. I have worked jobs just to pay the bills and let me tell you, it is not inspiring. It can open up the vortex of mediocrity. Do everything you can to avoid being sucked into that vortex, too. It starts with a job you don't like and a general lack of passion in life. It continues with constant complaining about that job, then spirals into complaining about other people. Then you hang around with those people – the wrong people - and start to make questionable decisions based on what is around you.

Welcome to the vortex.

You may even think that the world owes you. You may experience poor quality eating and lack of fitness, negative speak, and a complaining attitude and the above. If this is you, you have officially entered the vortex of mediocrity. It is here where you have to change your viewpoint and be a true champion for your own life, make some changes and don't look back. There is no rear view mirror in life.

CHAPTER 6

SHAPE YOUR CHARACTER

"Be more concerned with your character than your reputation, because your character is what you really are, while your reputation is merely what others think you are."

— John Wooden

Your character is shaped internally through your upbringing, usually first by your parents and then as you grow up, by the people you spend time with. The circumstances that you encounter along the road of life also contribute, of course. So, because you are constantly creating and shaping your character as you go, it's important to prepare yourself for any opportunities that might come your way and help shape who you are and who you might become.

Opportunities are like the bus – day in, day out, they just keep coming. If you have not shaped and forged your character and internal compass, you will not be ready when the opportunities come and the bus will drive right by you, or maybe even over you, if you aren't lucky. You will not realize the opportunities that can potentially make you who you are. You get to make who you are. It is your job to be "you."

You are the one who gets to create how you feel. It doesn't matter if you are a product of poor parenting. It doesn't matter if you were the smallest guy on the field – the one who never got picked for the team – and it doesn't matter if you once considered a nerd who got no respect from others in high school. Maybe you were shy back then - and maybe still are. All those things don't matter, not even a bit. What matters is your character today. Are you a good person? Do you respect others? Do your actions come from a place of love? Are you excited to see other people succeed? Are you a good sport? Do you compete fairly? Are you ethical? Do you make the right decisions? Do you stay out of trouble? Do you help others in need? Are your kind and gentle, and assertive when necessary? Do you have a great attitude? Do you protect people when others talk badly behind their backs?

How do you react to situations that are difficult? People with character always seem to be in control – and that's because they are. They are not in control of others, but rather, in control of themselves. People with character don't say negative things about others, they don't see problems where others often do, and they are thoughtful in how they act and speak. People with great character respond and do not react. You see, the way we react is often a direct reflection of how we saw our parents once react. Knee-jerk reactions are often caused by a built-in paradigm that we don't get to control.

Character must be forged like a blacksmith forges a horseshoe. It has to be shaped and smacked around a bit to become fully formed. Character must come under fire and be put under pressure to become whole. Typically, we have very little character when we are young. Character starts to form as we age, and when young, the character we build is usually a direct reflection of our parents and what we see through them. This is the part we can't control. We can't control how our parents behave, and what their level of integrity and character is. There will come a point if your life where you will start to think some of these things: Why am I reacting this way? Why am I talking about other people so negatively? Why am I judging that person? Why do I feel a certain way? Why am I angry about that subject or about what that person said?

This is primarily a reflection of your parents' influence. When you get to an age where you begin to take stock of yourself and begin asking yourself questions, start to look at your parents. Study them at home, see how they interact and see how they speak to each other and to other people around them. What will emerge is a picture of you. You are a direct extension of your parents. This age of realization is different for everyone – and dependent on all kinds of variables – but nonetheless, this realization is an important step to understanding yourself and shaping your own character. Remember, your character is yours only and cannot be blamed on something or someone else.

I would argue that our parents' era was steeped in character and integrity. They were from the "old days" where hard work was most important and a handshake agreement was as good as anything ever put in writing, and wouldn't be broken for anything. This was one of the brilliant things that my parents passed down to me along with a few others. "Be a man of your word," is a saying I heard a lot of growing up. This is a simple premise and such a trait is highly valued, and highly sought after, in any human being. We like to know that people will do what they say. If you go around in your day-to-day life saying you will do things but then you don't follow through, your character will be weakened or flawed in the eyes of others – and rightfully so. Having integrity is an opportunity to forge your character. Don't miss this opportunity.

I can tell you without a doubt that character is truly forged during difficult times in life. No one has taught me this lesson better than my good friend, Larry Clay. Larry once told me that it doesn't make any difference how "bad" things get. In fact, he told me to let them get even worse. This didn't make sense to me. He went on to explain that it will only make for a better story and you will appreciate the view from the top even better when you get back up there. Larry had gone through the valley of difficulty with such strength and courage that it was confusing to me and I didn't understand it at the time. After long discussions with Larry it became clear that you don't change who you are in difficult times and struggle but rather it is an opportunity to rise and create who you are.

Oh boy, was he right.

While winning is satisfying and something that we all want for obvious reasons, it is very easy to accept. We have no problem with it. We smile, we celebrate and we do it all over again because winning breeds winning and success spawns more success. It's the hard times that teach us the most, though.

Now, hopefully there aren't too many difficult experiences in your life to date. Maybe you're lucky so far and there have been only a few at best. Well, not to be alarmist, but let me tell you something – hard times are coming at some point. But the luckiest of us survive, we always do, in some way or another. And when the hard times arrive, they will provide you plenty of opportunity to forge and shape your character.

"Character cannot be developed in ease and quiet. Only through experience of trial and suffering can the soul be strengthened, vision cleared, ambition inspired, and success achieved."

— Helen Keller

You really need to know who you are or who you want to be. Ask yourself: who do you want to be and how do you want to behave? If you know who you are and what your core values and beliefs are, you will know how to respond based on this knowledge. When I asked myself this question, some time ago, my answer helped define my behaviours and daily habits, which in turn, made me who I am today. My answer to that question was that I want to be a solid role model to my children (a large part of parenting is just showing up). I want to be a man of my word – someone with integrity; be physically fit; grow my business; be kind and respectful to people; be philanthropic; and be a hard-worker who is dedicated to fulfilling my goals and dreams.

Once I knew who I wanted to be and what I wanted to do, the path I needed to take became much clearer. Without having an idea about who you want to be, you will twist in the wind and be at the mercy of every situation you are in. You'll be simply surviving day-to-day, rather than thriving – you'll be a human *doing*, rather than a human *being*.

If you are grounded in your ethics, morals, values and principles, you will be strong in these same situations. You will feel more comfortable as a whole person. It will be easier to find the right people to be with and they will be attracted to you.

No one intentionally creates hard times in their life – nor should they – and no one says to themselves, "You know what? I'd really love to go through a difficult valley in my life and see if I can make life really tough." As a result, when we do find ourselves in one tough situation or another, it's likely that we've never been in that predicament before, and therefore have no idea how exactly to react. We don't know what to say, what to do or how to dig ourselves out of it. What is our reaction to the difficult time? Oftentimes, the default reaction is a negative one, and we may tell ourselves some of the following things: "This will never change," or "why me?" or, "I can't believe this happened," or "I can't believe how badly I feel." Then, there is perhaps the most common reaction: "If _____ didn't happen, then I would be way better off."

In difficult times we can become confused, because it seems the world – in fact, the whole universe – is against us. Or not doing us any favours at the very least. What we do in these difficult moments is critical, because how we respond forms and reveals our character. Some people will react to negative situations with the aforementioned negative responses, or simply with anger and hostility. Others will respond in a calm, relaxed and solution-oriented manner. We all know both types of people. The difference between them is character. The people who respond with a smile, are relaxed and are genuine in their efforts to find a solution. Perhaps they have been in these types of situations before. They have likely spent plenty of time thinking about who they are and how they behave.

Then, of course, are the other people who just get angry, yell and shout and are generally out of control. Clearly, they haven't taken the time to shape their character. I know some of you are thinking that there are certain circumstances that require yelling or screaming. I understand the thought, but I disagree. It is my opinion that, no matter how dire something is, there are very few cases that require aggression and raising the volume of your voice to get someone's attention or to attempt to solve a problem.

I'm talking about the person who is notoriously negative. Most things that come out of their mouth are about someone else, or about a certain negative situation they were in, about how sore and tired they are, and/or how the world owes them something. They are constant victims of circumstance, they say. You don't want to be one of these people, let me assure you. With these mindsets your life will spiral down into the abyss of victimhood.

In order to avoid this pitfall, you must shape your character early in life. Take some hits, get knocked down, fail, get hurt and be disciplined. These experiences will allow you to build up your resiliency. You will have choices about how to react and respond. Every reaction and response becomes who you are. Be very aware of how you respond to the people and circumstances that are around you every day. Simply reacting – quickly and with little forethought – is not usually the way to go. Responding is. When you are using all of your skills and abilities to control yourself, the outcomes are more favourable.

About a year ago, while I was driving to my brother's house on the lake, I needed to merge left while there was a car right behind me. I merged in front of the vehicle and the driver slammed on the horn. He held it for five seconds and gave me the middle finger. Within a fraction of a second, adrenaline pumped through my veins and into my brain. My first thought was one that, in my opinion, showed a lack of character and was the "old me." I wanted to scream out the window and tell this guy to go to Hell, or maybe even motion for him to pull over and then, well, the fight would've been on. Yes, that's a reaction I had on more than one occasion when I was younger.

These are the moments when the world is testing your resolve and character. These are the moments when you get to show who you are. Let me tell you, the person that acts with solid, consistent and reliable character is the person people trust and rely on in the long run. It's a main characteristic of a champion. The world doesn't lift up the person who screams back and provokes a fight. The universe and your friends and colleagues will instead respect the person who shows good judgement, and is calm in difficult times – whether in an office setting, on the sports field or while driving down the highway. These are our true leaders. We trust leaders because they act consistently and honorably.

Let's go back to that scenario on the highway when I was feeling more than just a little "road ragey." Yes, I just made that second word up – let's just go with it. We all know it would have given me immediate satisfaction to follow through with the initial urge to defend myself by yelling at the other driver. But that moment would be fleeting, and certainly doesn't help build character. We react to the adrenaline rush by lashing out and shouting obscenities. If I had lashed out at this driver, he would have been essentially taking my energy from me. Our world today is too full people seeking immediate satisfaction. As much as that may feel like the right way, believe me – it isn't. We all like to think that our way is the right way – even in the heat of the moment – but all it often takes is a moment to pause and think about the situation.

A few years ago, when my marriage was going through something of a realignment, we went to relationship counselling for two years. One of the greatest things I learned from that time – aside from the fact that counselling is extremely expensive – was that I am only half as good as I think I am.

There is an inherent belief in all of us that we are pretty damn great. There seems to be a built-in mechanism that tells us we are living life the right way. I believe this is a survival instinct. It would not do us good to think poorly of ourselves. We wouldn't progress much as individuals and as a society. Life could be kind of depressing.

Once the relationship counsellor took me through the paces, I realized that I had a fair bit of work to do on many fronts. We tend to believe that we are always right, and that our beliefs or life paradigms are based on what we learned growing up. Unless you were hanging out with world leaders and philanthropists and CEOs of massive corporations when you were younger, you're probably not as well-rounded as you think you are.

So knowing that, you probably have some things to change in your life. Don't be the aggressive angry person just because someone cuts you off in traffic. Don't be the unbalanced person who allows every somewhat challenging situation to rock their world. Don't be an "energy vampire" – a term I coined to describe a person who stops the positive energy flow of others, sucking the life out of them. These people are everywhere. There you are feeling peaceful and enjoying a beautiful day when bam! - the parking attendant sees you coming, but still continues to write up the ticket.

Or maybe it's the government employee at the Department of Motor Vehicles who finds power in making you wait. They suck the life out of you because they have nothing better to do. You must avoid these people at all costs, or you must win them over quickly with friendliness or humour. These people should not be allowed to take your energy. Remember that your energy isn't for sale, and is certainly not free for the taking. You are not roaming the earth with a sign on your back saying: "The next person who wants to sap me of my positive energy just go ahead – it's all yours."

There is also a large physiological difference when one acts calmly as opposed to with hostility. When we react with anger to challenging situations, our blood pressure increases and our system is overloaded with the "fight or flight" hormones. We get angry and then we relive the situation in our minds for a better part of the day. We replay the event over and over in our heads. We revisit what happened, what we should have done or could have done differently. This is, effectively, a waste of your time. Anger will solve nothing other than, perhaps, give you the immediate satisfaction we are wired to crave. Our world is built on instant gratification, which is counterproductive to building a patient, loving and faithful character.

Take a look at yourself now and think about how you behave, how you react, the things you say and how you say them. Look at why you believe or don't believe certain things. You behave in ways and believe in things mainly because of what you saw and what you heard growing up. Yes, there is an age where we are all responsible for who we are and what we say, and we can't use our parents as an excuse forever. But these paradigms or ways of thinking have been passed down from generation to generation and are built into your subconscious. If you want to change your paradigms and beliefs, you must work at it. The reason why a majority of people don't break the cycle is because it takes a lot of work to understand yourself and reshape your beliefs. You must be prepared to look at yourself. You must surrender yourself to the idea that you are not right all the time and that you are – gasp! - even sometimes wrong.

My advice to you is similar to the advice I have given my two children, Caitlin and Braedon: Be fully absorbed in life. Find what you love to do and make every mistake possible. I will caution not to make the same mistakes twice because then it is not a mistake anymore, it is a decision. Mistakes are the only way you will become great. Dive into life, fall down, get hurt, feel the pain, but above all, keep getting up after you are knocked down. If you are truly passionate about something, getting knocked down is only temporary. You can begin to see your failures as requirements for success. It won't be painful – it will feel like you are actually making some headway. If you are not truly passionate about the endeavour, you will almost certainly let even a minor failure or roadblock stop you, and you will not be motivated to continue. This is why having a passion for your chosen endeavour is absolutely critical. If you truly love what you are doing, then you will let nothing stand in your way of seeing it through to completion. People are attracted to others who are passionate and determined. This is because having such passion for one's life purpose is unique. Those with passion shine, their passion is palpable. You can see it in their eyes and hear it in their words.

Be this type of person. Don't be a "still person" as I like to call them - still complaining, still broke, still out of shape, still going to bed too late, still unemployed, still someone else's fault, still everything but happy and peaceful.

Once you open up your mind to these ideas, you will soon see the massive possibilities in your life that are available to you. You will begin to see life differently. You will respond, not react, to life's circumstances differently. You will begin to see that there are many different perspectives from which to view any situation. One person can see a situation as bleak, while the other can see it as stroke of luck. Yes, you can both be right. There are many ways of looking at the same thing. Your perception or belief about a particular situation is simply your interpretation of the outside world. At the end of the day there is no right or wrong. There are just different ways of thinking, behaving and interpreting the outside world. And each way will yield different results.

Because the people you associate with have such an influence on who you are, it is imperative that you choose carefully who you spend your time with. At an early age, we want to spend time around the people that we have the most fun with. This is natural and normal. As young children, our parents wanted to make us smile and feel happy. Finding friends that make you laugh and feel happy fits well into this mandate. As we age, we need to be more selective regarding the people with whom we associate. The happy-go-lucky friend that we had as a kid is often not the right choice for a close friend in our teen years or adulthood.

Our chosen associates will either raise or lower our standards. They either help us become the best version of ourselves or encourage us to become lesser versions. We become like our friends. No man or woman becomes great on their own. The people around them help to make them great. We all need people in our lives who raise our standards, remind us of our essential purpose, and challenge us to become the best version of ourselves.

My best friend and roommate in high school and university, Tony McGee, and I were inseparable when we were growing up. We were friends from the time we were 14 years old, and still are to this day. I don't think it is possible for me to laugh and have more fun with anyone aside from my buddy Tony. We had the time of our lives in our late teens and early-20s. We skied, partied, played video games and really enjoyed our lives. Eventually, we knew that living together had to end and it became abundantly clear we weren't exactly perfect with regard to each other's growth in life. We knew that if we kept up our pace of good times, it probably wouldn't end well. We might end up broke, hurt or at the worst, dead. It was not because we didn't like each other anymore, we simply knew that we needed to move on and fulfill our individual purposes.

Just like your character is usually visible to others, so too is other people's character to you. If your friends are "downer" type people, speaking badly about others, saying negative things about others, then these are not the friends for you. Listen to the words people use. Be a person with a great vocabulary. There is nothing more eloquent, sophisticated and classy than a person with a good vocabulary. You may be wondering how this can be developed. First, grab your-self a thesaurus and read it when you have free time. When I was a child I read *Roget's Thesaurus* every night before bed - I read it cover to cover and many times. Secondly, when you hear an interesting word and don't know what it means, hit up the Google machine. Make sure you understand its meaning, then try to use it in a sentence over and over until it's part of your vocabulary. Like anything else it will take practice and time to develop a strong vocabulary, but what a fantastic weapon to have.

Or a *prodigious* weapon, if you will.

See what I did there?

CHAPTER 7

INVEST IN YOURSELF AND WATCH YOUR WORLD GROW AROUND YOU

I didn't make up the rules of life, but I can report what I have learned after over 40 years of effort, hard work and studying. You have to take care of yourself. This can mean a lot of different things to a lot people. If you truly want to be successful in all areas of life, there are a few things that you must do.

Let's start with the physical, our bodies. You have to get out and exercise. This isn't a new idea – people have been saying as for centuries, but now more than ever we realize how important this actually is. We must exercise our bodies in order to ensure they're working at full capacity, both mentally and physically. We don't need to be bench pressing 400 pounds or anything, but we do need to be getting regular exercise, whether it's in the form of a bike ride, soccer practice, rollerblade, jog or whatever. The reason behind this is simple. When you activate the body, the mind reaps great rewards.

If everyone got a little bit more exercise, we could put half the doctors in the world out of a job. James Allen writes, "There is no physician like a cheerful thought for dissolving the ills of the body and no comparison with goodwill for dispersing the shadows of grief and sorrow. To live continually in thoughts of ill will, cynicism, suspicion, and envy is to be confined to a self-made prison. But to think well of all people, to be cheerful, to patiently learn to find the good in everyone.... such unselfish thoughts are the very portals of heaven. To dwell day by day in thoughts of peace bring abounding peace to their possessor." [5]

But it's not just doctors who'd be out of a job if people started taking the stairs every now and then, it's also psychologists. Here are 20 wonderful psychological effects that exercise has on the mind, taken from the popular website 'PsyBlog':

1. Increases stress resilience

Studies on mice have shown that exercise reorganizes the brain so that it is more resistant to stress *(Schoenfeld et al., 2013)*. It does this by stopping the neurons firing in the regions of the brain thought to be important in the stress response (the ventral hippocampus). This may be part of the reason that exercise does the below:

2. Reduces anxiety

Exercise has a relatively long-lasting protective effect against anxiety *(Smith, 2013)*. Both low- and medium-intensity exercise has been shown to reduce anxiety. However, those doing high-intensity workouts are likely to experience the greatest reduction in anxiety, especially among women *(Cox et al., 2004)*.

---

[5] Allen, James, *As A Man Thinketh* (New York: JP Tarcher/Penguin, 2008), p. 36.

3. Lower dementia risk

Almost any type of exercise that gets your heart working reduces the risk of dementia. A review of 130 different studies found that exercise helped prevent dementia and mild cognitive impairment among participants *(Ahlskog et al., 2011)*. Regular exercise in midlife was associated with lower levels of cognitive problems. As well, participants who exercised had better spatial memory.

4. Escape a bad mood

If you want to raise your energy levels, reduce tension and boost mood, you can talk to your friends or listen to some music. But most agree that exercise is the most effective way to transform a bad mood into a good one *(Thayer et al., 1994)*.

5. Fight depression

Just as exercise fights anxiety, it can also help fight depression. One review of 39 different studies, involving 2,326 people, found that exercise generally provides moderate relief from *depression (Cooney et al., 2013)*. It won't cure it, but it can certainly help. The effects may be as great as starting therapy or taking anti-depressants.

6. Speed up your mind

Working memory includes what's in your conscious mind right now *and* whatever you're doing with that information. After 30 minutes of exercise, people's working memory can improve. There's some evidence that accuracy drops a bit, but this is more than made up for by increases in speed *(McMorris et al., 2011)*.

7. Consolidate long-term memory

The effects of exercise on long-term memory are some-what controversial. However, at low-intensity, one recent study has found that exercise can benefit long-term mem-ory *(Schmidt-Kassow et al., 2013; see: Exercise Can Improve Long-Term Memory)*.

8. Boost self-control

A review of 24 different studies on the effects of exercise on self-control found that a short burst of exercise provides an immediate boost to self-control *(Verburgh et al., 2013)*. Although regular exercise didn't show an effect on self-con-trol, a period of moderate exercise did allow people to take better control of themselves.

9. Help with serious mental disorders

Schizophrenia is a serious mental disorder often involving hallucinations, paranoia and confused thinking. Despite its grave nature, there's evidence that exercise can help for this. It's also thought to aid those dealing with alcoholism and body image disorder *(Tkachuk et al., 1999)*.

10. Reduce silent strokes

A silent stroke is one that seems to have no outward symp-toms, but does actual damage to the brain. Without know-ing why, sufferers can start experiencing more falls, memory problems and difficulties moving. Exercise, though, reduces the chance of these silent strokes by 40 percent. It has to be more than just walking or playing golf, though; things like jogging, biking, playing tennis or swimming are probably required to get the protective effect *(Willey et al., 2011)*.

11. Alzheimer's protection

In the most common form of dementia, Alzheimer's, the brain literally wastes away; closely followed by the body. Neurons and synapses are lost and the sufferer's memory, personality and whole being slowly, but surely, disappear. Exercise, though, provides a protective effect against Alzheimer's by helping to produce chemicals which fight the damaging inflammation of the brain *(Funk et al., 2011)*.

12. Improve children's school performance

Children who are fitter and engage in more exercise tend to do better at school *(Tomporowski et al., 2011)*. Incredibly, one study has found that the increased mental abilities of children who exercise make them safer crossing the road when distracted by their mobile phones *(Chaddock et al., 2012)*. There's a reason to get kids to exercise if ever I heard one.

13. Stimulate brain cell growth

Part of the reason that exercise is beneficial in so many different mental areas is that it helps new brain cells to grow. A study on rats has shown that, in response to exercise, the brain regions related to memory and learning grow *(Bjørnebekk, 2007)*.

14. Increase executive functioning

What psychologists call "executive functioning" includes all kinds of useful abilities, like being able to switch between tasks efficiently, ignore distractions, make plans, and so on. Reviewing many studies in this area, Guiney and Machado

(2012) find that exercise reliably improve executive function, especially in older adults.

15. Better sleep

The relationship between exercise and sleep is a little more complicated than most imagine. It's not necessarily the case that exercise makes you tired, so you sleep better. For example, one study on insomniacs found that 45 minutes on a treadmill did *not* make them sleep better that night *(Baron et al., 2013)*. However, the study found that exercise did help sleep in the long-term. Participants with insomnia who kept to their exercise programs over 16 weeks did get better sleep than those who did not.

16. Prevent migraines

Migraine sufferers are often afraid of exercise because it might bring on an attack. But a study has shown that exercise can actually help prevent migraines *(Varkey et al., 2011)*. Participants who took part in three sessions a week on an exercise bike for three months showed improvements equivalent to taking the latest anti-migraine drugs.

17. Stop smoking

Even something as simple as a short walk can help people give up smoking. According to 12 different studies (reviewed by *Taylor et al., 2008)*, people who take a brisk walk, or similar exercise, experience less stress, less anxiety and fewer withdrawal symptoms when trying to quit. The reason it helps is partly because it actually makes the cigarettes seem less attractive *(Van Rebsburg et al., 2009)*.

18. Reduce motivation to eat

People tend to think that exercising makes you eat more to replace the lost calories, but new research questions this. Recent studies have found that, after exercise, people show lower motivation to eat food *(Hanlon et al., 2012)*. Exercise may suppress appetite by decreasing the body's levels of ghrelin, which is a hormone that stimulates appetite *(Broom et al, 2008)*.

19. It's more fun than we predict

The final effect exercise has on the mind is subtle. We tend to predict that exercising is not going to be enjoyable, but we are often wrong about this. Research has shown that while exercising can be a drag at the start of the session, people soon warm to it. According to one study *(Ruby et al., 2011)*, people enjoy their workouts much more than they thought they would. This was true across the board for many people and applicable to both moderate and challenging workouts. *(http://www.spring.org.uk)*

So, give it a go, it really won't be as bad as you think. You might even grow to enjoy it.

Eating the right food is critical to maintain a fit and active body, along with an astute mind. The body and the mind are directly related. What you do to the body effects the mind and what you do to the mind effects the body. In order to be firing on all cylinders, you have to eat the right foods and in the right quantities. The majority of people don't eat properly and don't exercise as they should. This is why we see such a huge epidemic of obesity in the world. I can tell you without question that you are not working at peak performance if you are out of shape, eating badly and not exercising.

My diet and daily food intake provides an example. My diet contains very little fat and is higher on the protein side. I have been eating the foods below and following a meal plan for the past 10 years. I am by far in the best shape and physical condition of my life. I tend to make all my meals for the week on Sunday. I find that when I don't have pre-made food on hand, that's when I tend to buy food that is higher in fat, usually from a restaurant or drive-thru. I make and package all food into Tupperware containers and store them in the freezer. I pull out what I need each day, and when it's all finished I make the meals all over again for the following week. This does take some discipline, and cooking for two hours every Sunday can be challenging, but it's what works for me. With enough trial-and-error, you'll find what works best for you. Here is my daily food intake and routine:

- 5:30 a.m. – a shake of mixed berries, some yogurt, a banana and a scoop of protein.
- 9 a.m. - protein pancake, consisting of peanut butter, brown sugar, Kodiak pancake mix, banana, scoop of protein powder and egg whites.
- noon-1 pm – Lunch: either pre-made chicken, fish or steak, or pulled pork with quinoa.
- Nap between 1-1:45 p.m. Getting up at 5 a.m. every day can make you feel a bit "nappy" in the afternoon.
- 3 p.m. - avocado and something with a little bit of fat content, often hard-boiled eggs.

- 5-6 pm – dinner: turkey chili.
- 8-8:30 pm – Snack. Sometimes I will get a little bit "nibbly" later at night. The key here is not to have any junk food in the house, because you will probably eat it. Whenever there are chips or some kind of yummy junk food in my house I find it very difficult to leave alone. It is easily justifiable because it is, technically, just a light snack, but the problem with eating the junk food at night is twofold: 1). It counteracts the solid day of eating that you just had. and 2). It's like anything else - if you do it repeatedly, over time it adds up. In this case, it will add up to an increased fat intake and a breakdown of daily discipline. To this end, I will stock my house with peanuts or similar snack for my late-evening cravings.
- 9-9:30 p.m. - Bed.
- Up again at 4:45 a.m.

Eating the right foods will keep you in great shape and will have a fantastic impact on your brain and body chemistry. When the body and mind are working at optimal performance you are more alert and certainly happier. All of your quality characteristics will be front and center. You will feel great and the world will see you as the winner you are. The opposite of this would be being tired, overweight, and unproductive, like the people who are always complaining and talking poorly about others. Don't be this person. Be the disciplined one who has a great attitude even when things go wrong. Life isn't fair and will often not go your way or the way you think it should. Don't fret, don't complain – tell yourself this isn't a setback but rather a set up.

God, the universe, fate, destiny, whatever you believe, works in ways you and I have no idea about. "Keep the faith" is a saying that I have used many times. Faith is the movement that moves through our spirt and our form. When you are in troubled waters and life is difficult, keep the faith. Keep the belief that it will all work out. Always keep a positive attitude. My dad's favourite line was "keep the faith," and it's become one of my favourites, too.

Again, it's important to remember that your life will not go the way that you think it will. This I know for sure. You will have a vision or a belief in your head about how you would like it to turn out, and you will likely also believe that a certain path will get you there. And you *can* get there if you stick to it, but the path might not be the one you first envisioned. This is not a problem at all. It is expected, really, and should be embraced and even relished. When life doesn't go your way try not to let it get to you, no matter the situation - maybe you didn't get the job or the promotion, or your co-worker is talking behind your back, or perhaps you don't have much money and opportunities look bleak. I could go on and on. You are no different from anyone else. We all have these ups and downs, that's just the way it is. No one is immune to life's hills and valleys and I can tell you with absolute certainty that if you ask anyone who has gotten anywhere in life, there were struggles and defeats along the way.

Remember: these are learning opportunities. You must understand them and let them guide you through the rest of your life. Don't make the same mistakes twice and learn from the ones you do make. Remember, this is where you learn to create yourself and who you are. This is where you have to make difficult decisions about yourself and your future. Choose carefully how to behave.

> *"Failure should be our teacher, not our undertaker. Failure is delay, not defeat. It is a temporary detour, not a dead end. Failure is something we can avoid only by saying nothing, doing nothing, and being nothing"*
>
> *— Denis Waitley*

Wake up with determination and go to bed with satisfaction.

Getting up early is one of the hallmarks of successful people. It's not so much that anything accomplished before lunch is worth more than anything you might do after the sun goes down, but by waking up with the birds consistently, it shows you have dedication, drive and can stick to a routine, even if it's often much easier – and more instantly gratifying – to hit the snooze button, roll over and go back to sleep.

Getting up early does serve many purposes. It will give you extra time to focus on what you love to do. It will give you a superior feeling that you are getting up earlier than 95 percent of the world's population. It will provide you with the discipline to go to bed at a reasonable hour to prepare for the next day. This will also help you turn off the TV at night, thus ignoring all its negative or otherwise useless TV programming.

In my case, I started getting up early because I needed to manufacture more hours in the day. I run and own a lease finance company (www.assuredlease.com); have two children whose sports I coach; I play golf, write books, train for triathlons and participate in a number of other activities. I just couldn't get everything done in the hours I was making available to myself. I needed more, so I forced myself out of bed, and now, every day, I have three plus extra hours for myself. I'm at the gym by 5:30 a.m. and in the office by 9 a.m.

Years ago, I realized I had to change my evening patterns. I used to sit around, watching TV and generally wasting time each night. I'd eat junk food, then go to bed around 11 p.m. or midnight. I'd wake up sluggish, tired and unmotivated. It wasn't easy making this change but I knew that to be balanced in life, I had to be consistent. I had to develop a laser focus. There were many times I was tired in the morning. Something in my brain would tell me that it's okay to keep lying in the warm bed, instead of getting up and facing my day.

I realized that there is no way I wanted to lose the first battle of the day. If you win this mental wake-up battle, you will win the day. The problem, I knew, lay in my thinking. If for some reason I was to go to bed later than 9 p.m., I would tell myself internally that I was as going to be tired in the morning. Once I changed what I was telling myself instead to, " you will wake up fresh and invigorated with more than enough sleep", I began to pop out of bed. This is the difference I am talking about and can be used in any situation in life.

I think my dad appreciates my new routine more than anyone – or finds the irony in it, at least – Considering that he was always an early riser when my brother Eric and sister Tina were kids, and we would always tease him about getting up so early while we, and so many other people, stayed in bed. But my dad ignored our teasing, and went out there instead and hustled.

Set a routine like this – whatever works for you – and I think you'll quickly find that these extra early-morning hours will become the most productive hours of your day.

Most recently, I used my three extra hours daily to write this book, get in the best shape of my life, learn how to meditate and just focus on myself and my day ahead. I've found that it's become the most empowering time of my day, and I can certainly see why so many successful people own these hours in their life and don't give the time away.

We must take care of our minds.

We have between 50,000-70,000 thoughts per day. This means between 35-48 thoughts a minute, if you can imagine that. Quite often, these thoughts are negative. I don't know why, but we tell ourselves a lot of negative things. We postulate and capitalized about future situations that we will never experience other than in our minds. I had been doing this for a long time, but finally, I had to stop. It is the biggest waste of time and, and is not good for our health, either. The brain doesn't know whether what you are worrying about is actually happening or not. If you tell yourself over and over that you are no good, that you're a failure or whatever it is you tell yourself, it will turn out to be the case.

I have consulted hundreds of people on this issue and the answer is always the same. We tell ourselves negative thoughts because it is engrained in our nature. It is a built-in mechanism of the human brain. Some say it evolved from prehistoric times, when the potential for being hunted down and killed by some large predator was way of life. Cave-dwelling people would always be on the look-out for danger and would anticipate possible negative outcomes, out of fear of in death or injury, if nothing else. I imagine there wasn't much good coming from sleeping in caves on the ground while massive, meat-eating animals lurked nearby.

We know that we engage in negative thinking, and that we do it way too often, and now we know that it must stop. You are a champion just the way you are, with exactly what you have. Full stop. Don't be tricked by your Neanderthal brain into thinking differently.

It took me awhile to figure this out, myself. But this realization – that I had the ability stop negative thoughts – was the final piece of the puzzle for me in discovering what I consider to be semi-enlightenment. I'd always had a good attitude and positive outlook on life, and was always kind and compassionate. I worked hard, and my family was well taken care of, but I still wasn't at peace and full of joy. The negative thoughts were robbing me of the peace of mind I deserved. All human beings want peace and happiness, and to get to that point, one thing we need is a quiet mind – one that isn't racing all the time, thinking about negative things without even understanding why. We want to be able to wake up in the morning with a clean mental slate, put a smile on our face and say to ourselves, "This is going to be a great day and I can't wait to be part of it." We want a mind that is peaceful. This is how Tibetan monks are said to think, totally at peace in their mountain temples. They slow the mind down until they completely control its thoughts and energies. This is a very difficult state of mind to achieve, and it takes a lot of practice, but in the end, can be worth it.

The good part is that we don't have the move to India and live on a mountaintop for years just to get control of our minds to stop racing. We can do a lot right here and now.

Meditation

Part of my daily ritual is 10 minutes of meditation a day. I do this after my daily workout is complete and before I start work in the morning. At first, this might seem difficult and, well, that's because it is. You are used to having thousands upon thousands of thoughts each day, and now the goal is to have none. If you're like me, you will only be able to last mere seconds for the first couple of weeks. Hang in there, don't give up. What you will soon find is that you will gain an ability to achieve a state of non-thought, or ground zero. This is one of the most beautiful states of mind to be in. A calm resolve will wash over you that seems to put everything in perspective. Have fun with it, laugh at yourself because you can't stop thinking. Laugh at the weird and odd things that you actually start to think about.

Above all, stick with it – close your eyes and stay that way for 10 minutes trying to focus on something in your mind. Usually when you close your eyes, you will form shapes in the distance. I create the shape of a heart, and work to be in a place of love and calmness. Ground zero.

You'll hopefully find the results of this practice to be phenomenally beneficial, and eventually you'll be able to stop the negative thoughts from coming into your mind. You are a powerhouse and needn't think about yourself in a negative way. Believe me, negative thoughts still come into my mind, but they leave as quickly as they enter. I realized that they are just rubbish and have no room in my mind anymore. We need to think about ourselves as the great gifts and spirits that we are. Once you master this, you'll wonder how you ever let such negatively control you in the first place.

Have you ever heard the saying, *We are our own worst enemies*? This is because we are. It's time to stop this pattern, as it will not serve you well and will even do damage to your life.

Give yourself positive messages consistently. Tell yourself you are a champion, you are smart, you're full of love, and that you'll ace whatever it is you're trying to achieve. Do it now, and the world will stand up and take notice before you realize it. The universe rewards these efforts.

It will take time and you will need to work at it, but once it becomes a habit, the positive messages will flow continuously and you will be unstoppable. Your eyes will open and you will begin to live life on your terms and with open eyes. You will not miss who you were, and will instead focus on what you are supposed to have.

Our internal dialogue is one of fear, of thinking we are not enough – not pretty enough, not fast enough, skinny enough, tall enough or good enough. You need to get your mind flowing and moving in the right direction so you can have a complete, fulfilled, balanced and enlightened life.

That pretty girl you are afraid to ask on a date because you keep telling yourself you're not good enough for her? Well, there's every chance that she is just as insecure as you are. We are all this way, to varying degrees, and none of us are different than anyone else.

So be bold, and embrace what you can see in front of you. No one has ever achieved anything of significance while sitting on the couch all day then staying up late eating potato chips and watching Jimmy Kimmel. The universe rewards the bold, the person of character, the person who dares, the genuine and the faithful.

Don't get me wrong here, I'm not saying you have to be a Navy Seal with fastidious discipline and rigorous consistency to get the absolute best out of life. That kind of commitment would be great, of course, but overall, you simply need to make a few changes and better manage your daily activities. There is all sort of books on time management, but I don't think of it as managing time, but rather managing activities. We all have the same amount of time in a day. You need to figure out what you want and build your days around it.

Have a look at what I wanted and how I structured my days to meet my plan. First off, I wanted to be fit and healthy. This doesn't mean benching 400 pounds at the gym or suddenly morphing into a a runway model. I'm talking about something far more simple and attainable – simply working to get my heart rate up for at least 20 minutes a day while eating food that is reasonably healthy. The fitness industry is a billion-dollar industry with all sorts of available support in areas of motivation, diet, exercise plans, analysis and breakdowns. Let me sum in up in a sentence. Exercise to get the heart rate up for 20 minutes a day and eat healthy foods that are not high in sugar.

Guys, this isn't rocket science. I can hear the excuses now, and that's because I've heard them a hundred times – even said them myself at times. *I don't have enough time; my kids take up all my time; I have to work all day...*

I understand that life is busy and time is almost always at a premium, but let's take off the kid gloves here. It's not that you don't have enough time, it's that you're not motivated to *make* enough. It is easier to sleep in. It's easier to not prepare foods for the week ahead and instead eat poorly. That's perfectly okay if that is all you want. Remember, there is no right or wrong, and there are certainly no judges here on earth.

If you are sleeping in, eating poorly and feeling good about yourself, then God bless you, but this book probably isn't for you. This book is for those of us who want to create our very best life, and know that we are not there yet. This book is for those of us who have looked in the mirror and into our minds and said, "I can do better than this." It's for those who want to elevate their game, make a bit more money, have deeper relationships, and be more at peace. It's for those who want to be comfortable in the moment and accept the fact that they have some work to do.

Whichever way you are, you need to really love yourself immeasurably. If you aren't loving yourself and living your fullest life, then we've still got some work to do. Let the process be fun. Realize that it will take some time. It may very well take years to climb the mountain, but the choice is yours. How much does it matter to you? Does it matter only enough that you will quit in a month or two? That's okay if it does, no worries. But if it matters a lot to you, there will be no quitting. The obstacles and people that impede you will be swatted away like flies, and more than that, they will stay away from you as a vampire steers clear of garlic.

Your path will become clear and the opposite effect will happen. Other people will reach out to you. Other people will celebrate you and help you to the top. That is the way we are as humans. If you are hanging around with champions, they will do everything they can to lift you up, put you on their back and help you. We all need help at different times, so make sure you're around champions. Victims will only revel in your failures and do nothing to help.

I want to be fit and healthy so I can play with my kids, sail a boat when I'm 65 years old, and be able to keep going to the gym regularly for the next 20 years. The second thing I wanted to do was to write this book. Some other things I wanted to do were: continue to run my finance company that I have owned for over 20 years; take the first three hours out of every day for myself; continue to be a great father and role model for my children; and master my thoughts and be in control of my mind.

Basically, I want to have everything this world has to offer and I want it in abundance. I knew I was no different than anyone else, but I also knew I was entitled to this. I just needed to get organized, manage my activities and work consistently for years to get there. I want to remind you this will not come overnight. With very few exceptions, nobody gets to the top that quickly – there are very few overnight sensations. Scaling mountains is not easy and that is hopefully what you want to do in this life – scale your mountain. Climbing to the top of your game will take some courage, but it will be well worth the effort.

When your thoughts are pure, your circle of friends are a positive influence, you are consistently working towards your goals, you are overcoming negative mindsets, and your work is your passion and joy, you will begin to see life in a different way. You will begin to see people differently. You will begin to get the best out of life and life will begin to give you the best it has to offer. Your judgement of people will slip away, you will begin see things with a more open mind.

Let's face the facts here: we all see life in a way that was taught to us early on, and it's altered by what we learn along the way. I don't want to live life the way that I was taught growing up. I want to live life my way. I certainly want to take the good things I was taught growing up but I also want to get rid of things that don't serve me well. I want to purposely design my life the way I want it.

What this world has to offer is not a mystery, and like I've said many times, we all want the same things. In fact, we may realize that we already have several of these things in our lives, and we can have them all if we're willing to put in a little more work, be a little more disciplined and really start to care about ourselves.

When I was younger I heard the quote "The guy with the most toys wins." I used to believe that, because I had money on my mind and my mind on money. After a little experience and maturity, I don't believe this anymore. I still believe that money is important, but also that it affords you further opportunity to be of service to others. It affords you certain freedoms. I now believe that the person with the most peace and happiness wins, and it is from this peace of that everything else in life will flow. Peace of mind allows you to see the opportunities in life that may present themselves.

I have grown to understand that what we believe we want isn't always what is best for us, or necessarily what we need. Open your mind and open your heart if you want to have life's successes. Get rid of all of the stereotypes you carry around with you. Get rid of most of the information you learned growing up. Remove all of your paradigms that you have learned. We live in different times now and, often, old ways of thinking don't work anymore.

No matter your methods, there is enough room for everyone and there is enough of the pie for everyone, too. Think fullness, think equality, and believe that we are all the same. If someone else succeeds it doesn't mean there are fewer for you. You will get there, too; you just may not get there the way you thought you would. There are just way too many variables and too many possibilities in life for you to accurately predict exactly how you will achieve your goals. "Go with the flow," is a great saying, but I have since changed this to "Be the flow."

But the point remains, if you are flexible and realize that life doesn't always go the way you want it, you won't overreact, give up or stop expecting to reach your destiny.

Here is the rub: if you don't have a passion for something or don't have any goals in life, it will be difficult to adapt to unexpected changes. Here is the double rub: (if there is such a thing) if you don't have peace of mind, then it will be hard to continue. You'll feel beaten in your heart and in your spirit. This is why people become depressed and give up. They don't have any passion for their chosen endeavour, and they aren't going with the flow. They aren't realizing that other people don't know how they will get there either, they just know they will.

Life is not easy and is a constant test of will and purpose. What I am saying is, lean into life with the heart of a champion and a positive mindset. Know that life won't always go your way, and that that is okay. Finding something you love is at the heart of success.

"Doing what you love is the cornerstone of having abundance in your life."

— Wayne Dyer

If you don't care about what you're doing, you will most certainly not be very good at it. You may give up or quit when there is an obstacle. Champions don't give up or quit for two reasons:

1. They have a firm and entrenched belief that they will get there and complete their goals. They have commitment to themselves.

2. They know that it will be difficult and things won't always go their way. When it doesn't, it's no big deal because they were expecting it. Obstacles are a guarantee in life.

This is no different for any human being on the planet. Lets be honest, if getting to the top was super easy, it wouldn't nearly be as much fun when you get there. Embrace the challenges and obstacles and know they are coming. Who you become is based on how you responds to these challenges. It is that simple. This is how our lives are designed. Don't be a victim to life and let these challenges and obstacles beat you down. Have goals, have dreams, have an understanding of who you want to be and have a plan to get there.

I spoke in an earlier chapter about people who are victims in life, people who are always complaining and living with regret. Don't be this kind of person. These people have few goals or passions, they let the changing winds of life beat them down. Victims of life don't give thought to creating who they are. Champions aren't victims, champions are warriors. Champions have the same challenges as victims, but they just see them differently. They see obstacles as challenges, they see road blocks as hurdles to overcome and they see opportunity where victims see problems.

It is your job to be a champion. No one likes the victim. Victims don't elevate themselves. Their desire is the complete opposite of the champion; they want to bring other people down to their level so they feel better about themselves. Do yourself a favour, get these people out of your life. You may be saying, "It will be hard. I can't do that." The choice is yours, but these "friends" are not for you. Hang around people who are better than you. I can hear you saying it now, "But these are my friends I don't want to lose them." Well then don't, keep them and stay forever in the abyss of mediocrity. The choice is yours.

Ever since I changed this part of my life, I see and feel everything around me as full, happy and positive. My relationships with other people are full and rich. My business is running on all cylinders. The way I feel daily is inspiring. All clouds of doubt have disappeared. My fitness level is solid and my cash flow has increased dramatically. If your head is filled with negative thoughts when you go to bed then then you can't expect to wake up and see the world as one for the taking.

Take care of your mind and it will take care of you - if you do, the rewards are great. When you do this music will sound better, you will view people differently, you will hear the birds when they are singing in low tones, as if they are singing to you, and you will be seeing life through wide and enlightened eyes. The co-worker who you don't like will cease to be an enemy and will be a friend instead. You will let go of any bitterness, hostility or victim mentality. Forgiveness will be automatic. You will have no self-doubt. Don't walk through life with the blinders on, view your surroundings for what they are: beautiful.

You will have fantastic experiences that are full of joy. I am talking about continuous, daily happiness. You will have a smile on your face, and you will walk with a spring in your step that you didn't even know you had. The energy vampires will no longer exist. The people and situations that have caused the problems in your life will disappear. You will begin to live life on your terms. What you think and feel is the portal to your existence, to how you are perceived and, in turn, the opportunities you receive.

If you aren't where you want to be and you aren't who you need to be, then it is time to stop whining and complaining about your life and get to work on yourself! What are you really doing with the 24 hours you get each day?

Are you working on your skills, improving yourself, enhancing your gifts and talents, or are you just letting time pass and achieving nothing of value?

This is your wake up call to get to work and start doing the things you should be doing.

You have to do the work, no one will pay you to wake up earlier to work on yourself. No one is going to magically appear to pay your bills while you try to rebuild your life. You have to be self-motivated and disciplined enough to do what is required of you.

Some people may have the luxury of time and money to work out what they want to do with their life. Others may "find themselves" while they travel the world. But most of us don't, so we need to get to work. Use every spare minute you have to build and create the life you want.

You might feel like you don't have a lot of free time, but it's on you to make time for your own development and growth every single day.

CHAPTER 8

YOU'VE GOT TO WORK HARD

If there was one thing my parents always told me, it was to work hard. It's fairly common, straightforward advice, and seemed to make sense at the time. If I work hard I will be able to have nice things and live a decent to successful life. Perfect, sign me up.!!!

They stopped at that. Just go work hard. Now, does that mean I have to work long hours? Work hard doing physical labour, or anything related to those things? I had no idea at the time, as the advice, while well-intentioned, was not complete.

What they should have told me instead was to first find something I love to do – something that makes me happy – and work hard at that. They should have told me to go find a passion. When you find your passion, you will love it so much that you will want to do it all the time. You will do it just for fun. You will do it so much that you will become an expert at it. People will pay you lots of money for your expertise in that field, whatever it may be. Your life will, in turn, be filled with purpose and joy.

What a huge difference in philosophies. I was essentially told to get an education so I can go work for someone else and build their dreams. This is largely how society is structured.

Why didn't someone show me, at an early age, how to pay my taxes, or invest my money? Why weren't we taught to find a passion and to love something? Should we not be taught how to be peaceful and happy in our hearts? Quit teaching about us about parallelograms, quizzing us about state capitals and King Henry, and instead teach us about real life and how to succeed, how to invest and how to develop the characteristics of a champion. Teach us how to succeed in human relationships. If you want to study French in high school, then great. But many don't, and for them, there is no use for a second language (unless you're hanging out in the South of France, trying to get lucky). But there *is* tremendous power in knowing how to get along with other people – teach us that instead. Teach us how to be creative and to color outside the lines. Show us how to deal with Johnny when he is bullying us on the playground. Teach us the power of perseverance and discipline. Teach us how to set and reach goals.

You see, once you have the passion and the love for something it only grows and manifests. If you don't have passion for your work or your purpose, then you will not go after it with 100 percent commitment and desire. Make no mistake, it doesn't make any difference what you love to do or what your passion is. It could be that you love to shear sheep, walk dogs, play the flute, race cars, or carve totem poles. Whatever you love to do, you will do it more often and you will, in turn, do it so much that you will become an expert at it. It won't matter that obstacles get in your way, because you'll knock them aside because nothing will stop you. People with passion let nothing get in their way of success.

Nothing.

People search for passion more than anything else in life. What I am about to tell you will more than likely change your perception of passion forever. Our whole life we seem to be in search of the one passion that we think will bring us fulfillment. The concept of passion is usually based around a career or money-making endeavour. We believe that if we fail to find our passion we are behind the proverbial eight-ball or have some catching up to do. Well, guess what? No one who is passionate is only passionate about one thing. You can have passion immediately and in great quantity right now!

I would consider myself a passionate person. But I didn't wait to find the career or "get somewhere in life" before I decided to be passionate. I am passionate about being a great person, and about treating everyone as equals. I am passionate about my health and my family. I am passionate about being optimistic, finding the good in people, being a great father and having a good laugh amongst others. I have many passions in life. In all honesty, I didn't even consider educating and inspiring people a career. It is something that developed from a passion that I was already experiencing. I didn't just wake up knowing what my career or passion was going to be. None of the vast number of people I have met on my journey have known this either. If you don't practice being passionate in all the other areas of your life, you will never discover your true potential.

There is one great thing that all successes have in common. It is the passion for life itself. When you have passion for every part of your life, things fall into place.

If you are not passionate about what you are doing in life now, you will quit. Why? Because you don't really care about it. Let's all do ourselves a favour and find something we love to do. If we find it, and do it often, then it isn't really work at all. You often hear people say, "My job isn't work, I love what I do." You never hear these people complaining about their job, the commute into work or the people they work with. Be one of those people.

At 23 years old, with a degree in economics I went off into the world, armed with the information to work hard and nothing else. I had a crummy job, lived in a crummy apartment and no passion for anything other than sports, girls and having fun. Remember the saying "You can pay now and play later or play now and pay later?" I was playing now and it was because I hadn't formulated any type of plan for my life.

Being in this situation was very uninspiring and provided no source of motivation. Do yourself a huge favour and pay now so you can play later. You **can** be the professional at 26 years old earning hundreds of thousands of dollars. It doesn't take much to do this. It does take knowing what you want and it will take some hard work, failure and per-severance along the way. If you're already older than 26, then you can start now. It is never too late.

I think what my parents should have told me all those years ago was to work smart and hard instead of just hard. You don't need to put in 15 hours a day or work two jobs, unless of course you are building someone else's dreams. Instead, take a look at what is required to build your own. It is often way easier than you think.

So working hard isn't about manual labour for 18 hours day or working three jobs to barely equal the pay of one good one. Working hard could be better defined as finding something you love to do and becoming so good at it, so that your knowledge and skills are rewarded. Along the way, you will still have to "work." That is to say that you will need to stay up late, wake up early and log some long hours. But the difference is that you will do this happily and vigorously because you love it, not because you're being told to or have to. This is the magic of life's balance.

You must find something you love to do or have a passion for. Otherwise you will live your life without passion and, to me, that is not living.

CHAPTER 9

LOVE, PEACE AND HAPPINESS

Throughout our lives, we have all felt joy and happiness, love and peace – at least I hope that's the case. But we have also all felt, at some point or another, the exact opposite of this – pain, disappointment, unhappiness and suffering. Clearly, we enjoy the former much more – no one enjoys being angry and feeling bad and let's face it, being cranky, being a Debbie Downer, or a complaining, downright unhappy person just sucks for everyone – yourself, plus those around you.

By and large, most people stay away from these people. If you find yourself alone with very few friends, you are probably either introverted or are what I've referred to previously – an "energy vampire." There's nothing wrong with introverted – some of the coolest people I have ever met are quieter, more keep-to-themselves types. But just make sure you don't become the other option, where you end up sucking the life out people – where you're a drag, you're boring, you don't smile, and you tend to find the negatives in everything and everyone. You can find these people without really looking too hard – they're the ones who never get excited about something, never refer to experiences in a positive way, and their actions are often riddled with negative word choices, downtrodden body language, weak posture and negative emotions. If this is you or even close to being you, I am going to suggest that you take some time to work on yourself. You are going to need to make a plan to becoming a better person. Remember, you are your own greatest asset, and if you are not prepared to put in a little work then you will always remain where you are

On the opposite end of that spectrum, if you are already a positive person – if you've successfully kept all of life's balls in the air, and things are pretty good for you – well, then I say "Congratulations." That's no easy feat, and I know firsthand that getting to that place in your life is not easy. You've found your flow – the thing that allows you to find peace of mind and happiness, and makes you leap out of bed in the morning with a smile on your face.

And if you are one of these lucky people, you, too, know just how tough it was to get to that point in your life. You've found your passion, you've forged strong relationships and have a positive outlook. Now, your efforts need to be centered on keeping all these things without sliding back into old habits and negative mindsets. Keep that tempo up, continue your daily routines, and stay hungry for future success. Do not, under any circumstance, allow yourself to get complacent and think, "Oh, I've made it." You've advanced to a good place, for sure, and you have achieved many goals, but there are always more mountains to climb. Keep the pace, keep running.

The world has a cruel way of punishing the complacent, I've discovered. It has a way of balancing the playing field. In sports, it's often said that the only thing harder than winning a championship is coming back the next season and doing it again. In order to stay at the top, you need to work just as hard – or perhaps even harder – than you did in the beginning.

I used to think it was the guy with the most toys at the end who wins the game of life. I used to think the people who were most successful monetarily were the true victors. I have since changed my paradigm about this and am now convinced that it is the person who has the most peace of mind and the most joy and love in their lives who wins. The magic in having such things instilled in you is that once they're there, everything else falls into place: the money, the good job, the beautiful spouse, the "lucky break."

Love, joy and happiness only spawn more love, joy and happiness.

We all win and we all lose, and we all have ups and downs. The ability to live with eyes wide open in state of bliss –to be relaxed through the ups and downs – has been the hallmark of success for some of the greatest people in history, as well as plenty of people I have known personally.

"Don't get too high, and don't get too low," is something we have all probably heard a thousand times over the course of our lives. The winners know that whatever happens in their life, be it good or bad, they will be able to handle it and respond with great clarity and understanding. This takes the fear out of life – the fear that you won't get enough money, you won't have enough love, you won't get that promotion, and you won't find the man or women of your dreams. Peace of mind is knowing you will be okay in the end, no matter what.

Once you've achieved that state of being, you'll be surprised how relaxed you become, and how many successes may follow.

Always remember that Money is numbers, and numbers never end. If it takes money to be happy, your search will never end.

— Bob Marley

Celebrate the success of today, but also with the knowledge that tomorrow is just another step in your long quest forward. Take time to reward yourself, of course – every success deserves to be celebrated in some form or another – but don't let that stop you from challenging yourself to be even better.

Then there is, on the flip side, the "lows" – and this is where you really need to pay attention. These low emotions seems to have, unfortunately, a far more lasting effect on us than the more positive experiences. I don't know why that is, exactly – I guess we're just wired a certain way – but we do pay more attention to the downs than we do the ups, and in many cases, these down moments seem to circle us like vultures. They stay in our heads and affect us negatively. But once you're able to flip this mental process around and stay in the happy, calm and peaceful state of mind, you truly begin to see the world through a new lens. Your negative, biased opinions – about your life and the people in it – will slowly fade away, and give rise to the magic that will soon come. I think we can all agree that we prefer the happy, peaceful and joyful feelings way more than any negative ones.

So why not work as hard as we can to keep our minds in that former state, and push out the latter emotions?

The goal then becomes figuring out how to maximize the amount of time that you are at peace. I often speak of being blissful. To me this is the real goal. Blissful to me means being in a happy, excited state of mind with true warmth in my heart. For me, it is the feeling that you have a true purpose and are destined for great heights and something magical. It's a feeling that sometimes comes and goes, but it's what I'm always chasing, and the more I focus on attaining it, the longer the feeling stays each time I catch it.

"Every single being, even those who are hostile to us, is just as afraid of suffering as we are, and seeks happiness in the same way we do. Every person has the same right as we do to be happy and not to suffer. So let's take care of others wholeheartedly, of both our friends and our enemies. This is the basis for true compassion."

— *Dalai Lama XIV*

If we really want to conquer the world, we aren't going to be able to go into "action-movie mode" and do it by sheer force, blowing people up until we're left alone at the top. That plot might make for a good Arnold Schwarzenegger movie, but it's not reality (And that's probably a good thing, too). Instead, we will conquer the world with our love. Let us fill our lives with it, and it will be possible for us make it to the top.

We do not need to carry out exorbitant, grand plans in order to show great respect and love for both ourselves and our surrounding community. Instead, it's the small gestures – and the effort and intensity we put into them – that result in truly beautiful moments.

Both peace and war start often within one's own home. If we really want peace in the world, let us start by loving at home, within our families. Sometimes it is hard for us to focus on one another. It is often difficult for a husband to smile at his wife, and for the wife to smile at her husband. We must try hard to make even these, the smallest of gestures. Love those who are nearest to us, in our own family. From there, that love spreads to whoever may need us.

I've found that it can often be easier to love those who live far away, but it is not always as easy to love those who are right next to us. It is easier to offer a dish of rice to meet the hunger of a needy person afar than to comfort the loneliness and the anguish of someone in our own home who does not feel loved. I want you to go and find the poor in your house. Above all, your love has to start there. I want you to be the good news to those around you. I want you to be concerned about your next door neighbour. Do you know who your neighbour is? These days, many of us do not.

When you want to be loved, love more, when you want to be happier inside, be happier outside, and if you want more money, spend time being valuable. Whatever it is you want, you must exude those qualities that are associated with it. It is simply impossible for you to get something you are not thinking about getting.

Be what it is you want to have. The energy flows where the mind goes.

Be positive, be happy, be content. Isn't this exactly what we want? Of course it is. We have all seen the person who is happy, smiling and enjoying him or herself. We often tell ourselves that person looks happier than I am. We may ask ourselves what they have that makes them so happy. We think they must have more "things" in life – more love, more friends, more money, a bigger house, a faster car…

We must all realize that it makes no difference what other people have. I can assure you that the person you are envious of is only happy because they have chosen to be this way. Well, guess what, you can be that happy. Start with putting a smile on your face, put on some music that makes you happy, say a few nice things to yourself, and feel love in your heart. Bam – you're on your way. You will begin to feel prosperous, you will begin to feel the love that is surrounding you, even if it isn't there right now. What will begin to happen is the universe will start to work in tune to the nature of your song. It will then manifest because that is the way you feel.

The key is to maintain this contentment throughout the day and throughout your life. I will say this again, a monk will spend his entire life trying to reach enlightenment. You can reach enlightenment if you do the above suggestions. Take away the noise, focus on the positive, change your thoughts and you will see a real shift in your heart and your mind. Life is meant to be fun and enjoyable, not an everyday struggle.

Embark on a mental state that will provide, above all else, peace of mind in any situation. Strive for a real and genuine feeling of joy and an internal desire that is filled with passion and drive. You must feel these emotions on a visceral level before they can be truly seen by the world and the people in it.

CHAPTER 10

TIME MANAGEMENT VS. ACTIVITY MANAGEMENT

We all have the choice to do whatever we want with the 24 hours given to us each day.

Sure, we all have responsibilities that somewhat limit our choices – most of us, for example, have to spend a number of hours working each day – but we still do have choice – including a choice to do absolutely nothing, for better or worse. I have children, and I have been a child myself, so believe me when I tell you that I know exactly what it looks and feels like to do nothing – to have relaxing on the couch as your only daily "goal." How many times have we said to ourselves that when we finish our exams or our difficult work week that we're going to kick back and chill out for a while — maybe sit on the beach and drink a few beers. Or, once I finish this project, I'll relax and take some time off.

Most people want to enjoy some relaxation after achieving something, and there should definitely be rewards along the way. Sometimes this might include sitting around on a beach, having a few cocktails and eating with family and friends. This is great, because soon enough, you're back in the real world, working hard and achieving new goals. What is not as great, however, is simply coming home from work each day and watching TV until midnight, while your brain justifies the action as something you've earned. Sure, have a night or two like that on occasion, but it's a problem when it becomes a daily routine. Once it becomes a habit, you start to feel awfully tired in the morning, and your day suffers as a result. I've done that, guilty as charged. There was a point in my life, many years ago, where I would come home after a long day of work and want nothing more than to watch Jimmy Kimmel, David Letterman and the news on TV, until I eventually went to bed around midnight or later. In fact, there would be times where I would even watch the same newscast twice – the same ridiculousness over and over. On top of this, I would get up in the morning with just enough time to brush my teeth, put on clothes, throw some food down my throat and rush off to work.

Eventually, when I looked at how I spent my 24 hours each day, I realized that I was effectively giving my time to someone and something else. I was doing nothing to better myself. But at the time, I was so focused on the here-and-now – just surviving – that I just didn't see the problem. I didn't recognise that I was building someone else's dream. I had sold myself out, as they say. Sure, I was getting paid, this was most certainly the best part of what I was doing at the time. As much as money is important, it is more important that we obtain money in a way that is fulfilling. This is why developing a passion for something you love is critical.

Imagine there is a bank account that credits your account each morning with $86,400. It carries over no balance from day to day – every evening the bank deletes whatever portion of the balance you failed to use during the day. What would you do? Draw out every cent, right? Each of us has such a bank inside ourselves – The First National Bank of Time. Every morning, it credits you with 86,400 seconds. Every night it writes off, as lost, whatever portion of this you have failed to invest wisely. It carries over no balance. It allows no overdraft. Each day it opens a new account for you, each night it burns the remains of the day. If you fail to use the day's deposits, the loss is yours. There is no drawing against tomorrow. You must live in the present, invest the day's deposit properly so you can enjoy the utmost of health, happiness, joy and success. The clock is ticking, so make the most of all those seconds.

There is a big difference between time management and activity management. No one can manage time because the world revolves around the earth every day the same way. We get light in the morning and darkness at night. You can't control or manage time itself. What you can do is manage the activities of your day within the time we are given. We are all working from the same clock, so be very careful how you choose to manage your activities. Your daily activities will affect how you feel, what you have, what you think and what impact you have on the world.

Let's face it, getting up just in time to get to work, working all day for someone else, coming home knackered and sitting on the couch until bedtime – then doing it all over again the next day – will not get the job done. Remember what I said earlier, you are by far your biggest asset, so you need to spend time managing your best asset: yourself.

The more you work on and improve yourself, the more valuable you will become to yourself, others, and society as a whole. Take a look around and ask yourself what kind of an impact you are having on yourself and the people around you. Again, if you are all you want to be, and already have it figured out, then congratulations. But if you're like the majority of us, you will likely want to change some things. You may want to be more productive and have a more positive impact on yourself, your community and the world at large.

When you manage your daily activities, you get to be and do exactly what you want. First, ask yourself what your passion is, what you love to do. For me it was to spend more time with my children, work on myself, read more books, meditate, grow my business, get really fit, write this book, do my second triathlon, complete my website www.bruceellemo. com and learn to sell physical products online. That was how my plan started. I have the same 24 hours as you and I knew I was going to need some time to complete these tasks. Make your plan and life a great one, don't settle for mediocrity.

"So many of our dreams at first seem impossible, then they seem improbable, and then, when we summon the will, they soon become inevitable."

— Christopher Reeve

Once you have your plan, you're going to need to figure out your daily activities. If going to work is one of them, then you can take eight to nine hours out of that time, leaving seven of your 16 waking hours left. Take two hours out for cooking, showering and eating. That's five hours a day, multiplied by five days a week. There are four weeks a month, 12 months a year, for the next 20, 30, 40, 50, 60 years, depending on how old you are. Let's say you are 40 years old-old and will live until 80. This, of course, is for discussion's sake only, because the way modern medicine is evolving, you will probably (hopefully) live longer than that.

But let's use that example anyway. From that originally five hours of free time we decided upon earlier, let's take another two hours off because we have kids and "other" things to do. That leaves us with three hours each day (not including weekends) to do as we please. I can hear some of you now chuckling. "As we please? Ha! I have kids, a job, a spouse and house to run…"

Well, those are excuses. Welcome to life, we all have these things to do. Either make the time to increase the quality of your life or don't. If you don't want to spend these hours on yourself at least tell yourself that you aren't cut out for habitual, consistent hustle and hard work. Be honest with yourself, there is no shame in saying I'm just not ready to improve myself and am happy with things the way they are.

Here is all I ask, if you are the above person: Don't complain about it or whine about it to everyone you know. We don't want to hear how sore your back is, how tired you are, how you argued and told off your co-worker or how much of everything you lack.

But if this isn't you, then you want to make some positive changes so that you don't come to the end of your lives with any regret. Most of us want to take some chances. We want to achieve more and love more. We want to be more at peace, be more authentic, be friends to more people and be a better person overall. That's what I want, and I am certain if you are reading this book then you want these things as well.

So let's to get work on the three hours you have "given" yourself each. This is three hours day each day, five days a week for 40 years = 28,800 hours. This may shock you, but this equals 1,200 days, or 3.287 full years of extra time to work on yourself. Can you imagine all of the things you will be able to do with 3.287 years of free time? All you did was take time for yourself. All you did was to say that you are your most important asset and the time has come to really take care of yourself. You can have a life that is second to none, a life that leaves no stone unturned. Surely, when you think about freeing up 3.287 years of free time in your life, you must be excited. I will remind you that this assumes you take every weekend off. I always ask people to have a look at their circumstances and their bank balance to see if they can afford to chill on the weekends.

The above is exactly the reason you must manage your activities. You can accomplish a lot of things if you simply commit to yourself and to managing your activities.

This has helped me develop into my best person. My "best person" is someone who: has peace in their heart and mind; lots of joy in their life; is happy as often as possible; comes from a place of love; loves and respects people and the world at large; is compassionate; leads well; works hard; is focused and disciplined; and makes people feel better after being around them.

I realize that there must be some flexibility here because of kids' concerts, Little League baseball games, work activities and other such things. Not to mention things that pop up unexpectedly. But the key takeaway here is to have a plan that you stick to 95 percent of the time to develop the disciplines needed to change yourself. The other thing I hear often from people is that they don't have the time at night to work out or go to the gym. This is the time where we are typically the most tired from the day's work and the decision to go to the gym is the activity that almost always gets cut from the roster. The only other option in this case is to go in the morning or at lunch. That might seem like a challenge, but you must manufacture time, stay consistent and disciplined. Make up a schedule that works for you. You get to make the rules. You are the one who creates your life, so design it your way. The absolute key is to stay disciplined and stay consistent. Yes, it will be hard at first to get up at 5:00 am, and yes, you're going to be a bit sore, but suck it up. Go to the nearest cancer clinic and check in on how sore some of these people are. You'll be just fine.

Guys, it really depends on how badly you want the change; how much you want to be a better version of yourself; how much you want the success; how much you want to feel good every day; how much weight you want to lose; how much you want whatever it is that you want.

> *"The only way we could remember would be by constant re-reading, for knowledge unused tends to drop out of mind. Knowledge used does not need to be remembered; practice forms habits and habits make memory unnecessary. The rule is nothing; the application is everything."*
>
> — *Henry Hazlitt, Thinking as a Science*

By simply saying to yourself that you are important enough to invest in and giving yourself three hours a day to improve, you are opening the gateway to a better and inspiring life. Be inspiring, people will follow suit and the universe will respond. You don't need to know how; you just need to know it will. Lead by example and your kids will follow, too, which is never a bad thing. Commit to yourself and you will open doors that you never thought possible. You will see the world and the people in it in a new light. This commitment will also serve as an anchor for your life. When times get hard and you want to give up, or you just get tired, this anchor of personal commitment will serve you. It will help you get through the valleys of life that come your way, the troubled times that are inevitable.

When we have made this personal commitment to a routine or plan, the lows or valleys won't be nearly as low as they once were. You won't allow yourself to stay up in bed for hours mulling over what you should have said to your co-worker at work. There will be no more sleepless nights over your kids' unruly activities. The negative thoughts that were ever-present in your mind will slowly slip away, and when they do come, they will leave as easily as they came in.

The way you respond to people, and the way you talk to people will change. The way people look at you and respond to you will change. The energy or vibration that surrounds you will change forever. You will feel empowered.

Let me give you a great example of one of the ways it changed for me. I go to the gym a lot. Inside the gym there are a lot of people walking by, because my gym is a busy one. For years, I would avoid eye contact when I walked by people I had seen over and over. We all know the move – you look down as you are walking by someone in order to avoid eye contact and awkwardness. I had been seeing the same people every morning in the gym for years and never said, "Hi." I thought I would change this around and see what happens. Instead of intentionally missing an opportunity to communicate, say "hi" to people and learn their names.

Off I went to the gym each morning. At a minimum, I would say "good morning," with a smile, to everyone I passed. If I was working out beside someone I had seen many times before I would introduce myself. I intentionally used the same line over and over to see what the responses were. As a note, you don't want to be the "annoying talking guy" in the gym. My line was "Hi, my name is Bruce, I have seen you a thousand time in the gym." I would say it all with a smile or simple eye contact conveying warmth. Every response was identical. "Hi Bruce, I'm 'so-and-so,' a pleasure to meet you, and, yeah I've seen you in here a bunch." I would then say "Take good care" and continue to workout. What I would do from there is make sure I remembered their name. There is one thing I hear a lot in my life, it's "I'm not good at remembering people's names." This is probably the most important skill and one of the most underrated. Simply repeat the name to yourself after you heard it. If you get to the end of the conversation and you've already forgot their name, ask them one more time and then repeat it a few times in your head.

When you see the person again in the gym or wherever, greet them by their name. You will simply be amazed at how swiftly the friendships and acquaintances will blossom. When I go the gym now I literally have the names of every-one whom I have met in my back pocket, ready to go. I have some of the most wonderful and enlightening conversations with people who were literal strangers just days before. The greeting went from "mornin'" to "Good Morning Bruce, how are you today?" - all with a smile. Life is so much better when you start your day with your chin up, your head held high and you greet people with smiles. This attitude carries on and has a positive ripple effect through your day and ulti-mately, your life.

If you know who you are, you will find a way to exercise who you are in your daily habits. If you recall, part of who I wanted to be was happy, joyful and peaceful. As I am an extrovert, my happy place was meeting people, hearing their stories and having a good laugh. I got this fix through the gym and though my job. There is no longer room for people who don't fit this mandate of who I am. I incorporated a rule a while ago and it is as simple as it gets. "If it doesn't make me happy, make me money, make me better or come from love, I have no interest in it."

This habit really helped me get out of my judgement zone. If you have ever heard the saying "Don't judge a book by its cover," then try applying it to people. People on the inside are almost always completely different than you would have guessed based on your visual perception. The guy driving the beat-up pickup truck with long scraggly hair and a piece of straw hanging out of his mouth may not be the poorest guy, but the richest guy. The heavy-set guy who is always at the gym might not be trying to lose weight, he could be training for his 14th triathlon. The lady at the gym every day did not just got separated from her husband and wants to tone up, she is recovering from cancer and has been happily married to a fantastic man for 20 years. You get the point. We judge people in our minds, and this is just how it goes. Don't do it, it is another fantastic waste of time and energy and besides, you're usually wrong. Everyone is just like you, with a story to be told. They have victories and losses, like you. They have the same makeup as you. Don't think for a second that you are above or different from them, because you are not.

When your eyes are wide open, any judgement you have of people falls away. Any preconceived ideas about people that we so falsely generate in our own minds, fall away. All of the flaws that you have learned from your parents fall away and you can really begin to shape your life without boundaries. The best part is that the energy vampires will simply fade away. Negative situations and people won't find you anymore. A lot of life challenges and problems will simply disappear.

Once you create a proper mindset, it will guide you to who you are and who you want to be. Once you begin to really focus on your internal mandate and who you are, making daily life decision become second nature, and you'll be able to better use the limited extra time you have in the day.

It'll all begin to add up, second by second, minute by minute, and before you even realize it, you'll be a much-improved person.

"Cherish your visions and your dreams, as they are the children of your soul, the blueprints of your ultimate achievement."

— Napoleon Hill 1883-1970

CHAPTER 11

IT'S A PROCESS... THE COMPOUND EFFECT

When aiming to achieve a goal – any goal – the rules and the process in which that goal is achieved is, when it comes right down to it, no different for any of us. Sure, each scenario is different for each individual – and the goals of said individuals vary greatly, too – but by and large, we all have to follow a process.

There is no quick-fix solution nor a magic genie in a lamp that will help you get where you want to go. It takes a plan and hard work. Figuring out exactly what that plan is, and then taking the appropriate steps to execute, is the tough part.

The problem with most of us is that we often think of these things we want – a new job, a bigger savings account, building a business or a happy, stress-free retirement – but we never actually get started on the process that leads to these things. Why? Well, I'll tell you.

From the moment we are born, our parents tell us we can do anything we set our minds to. Those little giggles and coos coming out of your mouth at 18 months? Keep making them, keep trying, keep going and eventually you'll speak. There are no real other options – keep talking little Johnny. Keep pulling yourself along the floor until you learn to crawl, and then keep crawling until you can walk. For all these steps, your parents offer you endless encouragement – keep going and it will be done.

Notice the word 'will' there. Even if, as a baby, you have no idea of the concept, it takes *will* to learn to walk, especially considering how many times you will fall down in the process. It takes an enormous amount of will and determination to continue trying something that you've failed at previously. But we do it, because we're encouraged to do so. Eventually, we all pull ourselves up, and take those first few steps.

It is when we get to kindergarten that the rules begin to change and we are told differently. No longer are we encouraged in quite the same way – that way that suggests we can do just about anything. Sure, young schoolchildren are encouraged in some ways – often in that clichéd way that television characters are told that they can one day be President – but just as often, we're taught to play be a new, more-strict set of rules.

We're told not to colour outside the lines, not to talk when I'm talking, not to muck around – conform, just like the other children are taught. As so many of us fall in line, like little Sally, who is quiet and never seen as a bother.

There is a fine line between being creative – stretching our newfound wings – and becoming a disturbance, of course, but for many of us, these new rules are stifling, and we're completely shut down lest we're determined to be a nuisance and sent to the corner where we're told to think about what we've done wrong.

As we grow up and move beyond such elementary-school concerns, we are still, in many ways, taught to mitigate the risks in our lives. Think back to your high-school days, and try to remember what you were told back then. be careful; don't do this; don't be like that; I'm not sure that's a good idea; what is your Plan B?

It's all well-meaning advice sent your way by those who do not want to see you fail, which, when you really boil it down, is a far cry from those days as a toddler when you were encouraged over and over again to let go off your mother or father's hand and try to walk on your own, even if it meant that nine times out of 10 you were going to fall flat on your face.

God bless my father, whom I love to death and has always been the best dad a son could ask for, but risk was never his thing. When it came to risk – which usually showed itself in the form of an investment opportunity – my dad would pass, and through the years, would often retell the stories of those opportunities he'd pass up. More often than not, the tales would end with him saying "I'm sure glad I didn't invest that money with them. They haven't done a thing and I would have lost all my money."

On one hand, it's good that my father never lost the family savings by throwing our money at some fly-by-night operation, but it also planted a foundation that was unconsciously passed down to his young audience: risks are never worth it.

It's scary to take risks of any kind, of course. What if it doesn't turn out the way we want it to? What if we lose our money? What will happen if we fail?

All valid concerns, but what about the other side of the coin? What if we succeed?

Give your brain enough time to consider every single possible outcome, and you can talk yourself into, or out of, literally anything.

No one knows what the outcome of anything will be. The future is uncertain – that's the beauty of it – so don't let anyone else, even your parents, tell you what will happen. They're just like you – they're not sure, either.

This is why it is your job, and yours alone, to start the process of getting where you want to go. Instead of listening to people tell you how things will play out, start the process and *show* them how it will turn out instead.

It's a process I've tried to incorporate when raising my own children.

In many ways, I never put too much pressure on them, and tried to focus on teaching them core values – and the reasons we make the decisions we do – rather than focus on behaviour. I was very careful not to micromanage them – even if it meant they made mistakes along the way.

Believe me, if I could simply feed them life lessons intrave-
nously, I would have, but that's not how things work. They
have to walk their own paths.

After a certain age, for example, I didn't manage their bed-
times. I'd go to bed at 9 p.m., and I told them to go to bed
by 10:30 p.m. at the latest. Of course, and this will come as
no surprise to any parent out there, they were likely rarely
in bed by that time. They got to go to bed when they wanted
to – that way they'd know what it felt like to wake up tired,
and go through the entire day feeling sluggish and fatigued.

As human beings, we always want more and are designed
to want more, and I knew that at some point, being tired
each and every day would not be good enough for them and
they'd choose on their own to go to bed earlier. Sure enough,
that's what happened.

More recently, I was driving with my kids when my 15-year-
old son told me he wanted to start a more rigid, new daily
routine. He'd become disappointed in himself, he said,
because he seemed to spend way too much time watching
YouTube videos and playing video games, and generally
seemed to be wasting too many hours in the day.

I sympathized with him – I'd felt this same way many times.
When I was younger, I'd spent far too many nights staying
up too late, sleeping too much and just wandering through
life without a plan. Sure, I was getting up in time for work
every day, but looking back, I was just going through the

motions. I was letting the day dictate to me how it would go, rather than me dictating and owning the day.

I'm a big believer in the idea that I can try to motivate people as best as I can, but if they don't want to receive the motivation, there is nothing I can say or do that will make them want it. Inspiration has to come from within, and here I was sitting a few feet away from my son, who finally wanted it.

I'd been waiting for this breakthrough with him for a long time. It was difficult, at times, watching him sit in front of his PlayStation at 2 a.m., knowing he'd been there for hours.

Without a daily plan – without following a process – you're just surviving, I told him. I spoke the entire car ride and I could actually feel that they were listening to me and absorbing what they were hearing. What I said to them that day is the same thing I'd say to anyone. That is, that there are only so many things available to us as human beings – whether it's me, their mother, a teacher, or the guy in the car next to us at the stop light – and we are all the same in that we want certain things. We want love, happiness, joy, peace of mind, personal development, good health, money and often material items, be they a new house, nice condo or the latest iPhone.

Being a human being here on earth – and in Canada, no less – meant they'd already won the lottery, I told them, so it was important not to waste the opportunity they were given, as millions of people across the world would gladly trade places with them, given the chance.

My children had other benefits aside from simply existing, of course – another point I drove home during my car-ride speech. Neither child had pulled their headphones back over their ears, so I continued.

They are compassionate, smart, athletic, funny, attractive people with all cognitive functions – they had 10 fingers, 10 toes – and if they started to look at life with that in mind, every day would become a joy and a blessing. No one is immune to hardship, however, and no one coasts through life with ease, and that's OK, I said. But considering all their advantages, any tense moments were simply temporarily roadblocks to be overcome – tough times that would build character and strength.

At that point, I realized we were nearing our destination, and even though both children appeared to be yearning for structure, I was running out of time if I wanted to teach them about the process.

I stressed the need for discipline and the development of positive, daily habits – make your bed, put your dishes away, keep your room clean and closet organized, have a regular bedtime, eat healthy and keep a regular homework schedule. And for my son, one more piece of advice: play fewer video games.

Much of the specific advice I gave won't surprise other parents – it's much the same advice you've probably all dispensed at some parenting point or another. But in waiting for the right time – that exact moment where my kids *wanted* to hear it, it had a positive, lasting effect.

That's how the process got started for them. For others, starting a similar process could be a path to just about anything you desire – personal wealth, a new job, a new fitness regime… or maybe you just want to cut back on the hours you spend playing *Call of Duty*.

It's the people who never start this process who are instead hamstrung by doubt and what-ifs. Without a process, you'll lie awake in bed for hours talking yourself out of your dreams. Believe me, when you're under those sheets starting up at the ceiling fan, you'll come up with all types of justifications and reasons for why you can't do something. Maybe you don't have enough money, or maybe something is too hard, or requires you to wake up too early. Or perhaps you don't think you're good enough, or smart enough, or pretty enough.

Keep letting those thoughts override your goals, and you'll never get anywhere. Your dreams will remain just that – dreams. With that outlook, you're defeated before you even get started.

Instead, you need to realize that now – yes, now – is the time to rise up and create the life you want for yourself. Reclaim the magic of your childhood, and you'll be amazed at how life opens up for you and gives you everything you need. Once you drop that veil of "I'm not good enough," you will be steered in the direction of your dreams quicker than you ever thought possible.

The process:

1. **Start to be happy and grateful all the time.** How often have you heard of sad, ungrateful people making it all

the way to the top of their chosen field? Not often, right? Why? It's simple – because nobody wants to listen to them, or even be around them. If you are not happy and have a clouded mind, it will be very difficult for the universe to align itself for you. Being happy and at peace is a pre-requisite to begin the process. If you aren't quite there yet, try to put yourself in happy circumstances and surround yourself with happy, positive people – this is key. Being in a more positive environment will put you into a mindset of creativity and happiness. Do whatever else you need to do in order to achieve this state of mind – watch a happy movie, go to places you enjoy, go to the gym, your favourite restaurant, or grab a drink with a friend. Be happy and begin to see life as the blessing that it is.

2. **Get rid of all the negativity from TV, radio and elsewhere**. Just turn it off! You can't afford to be surrounded by so many negative messages and these days, they're everywhere. Yes, there is news out there in the world that is negative and at times heart-breaking – every day, people are killed, oppressed, buildings are blown up... you know all this already, so why allow even more of these messages into your life when they are contradictory to your goal of peace, happiness and joy? Get rid of anything – and anyone - negative in your life. If it happens to be a family member, make a point to spend less time with them. Be wary of their advice, too, should they offer it.

3. **Don't worry about what other people think.** This one bothers me most of all and I know it all too well.

But follow this suggestion and I can assure you that it, more than anything else, will provide you relief and the peace of mind required to elevate yourself.

4. **Eat properly.** Make sure you eat enough, and are providing your body with enough energy in order to get through the day without feeling sluggish and tired. Good health is the epicentre of your overall well-being.

5. **Invest in yourself.** Find good books related to your goals and desires, exercise, meditate, sleep well, and come from a place of love.

6. **Make a plan and stick to it**. Get up early. Get at it. You have to have a plan. Have you ever gone on vacation and not known where you are going? Of course not. Enough said.

7. **Stick with it. Stick with it. Stick with it.** Repeat, repeat, repeat – for years. There is no other way. Never under any circumstances give up on your plan or dream. Napoleon Hill's famous book, Think and Grow Rich makes it very, very clear that the number one reason why people don't succeed is because they gave up too early - right before the magic opened up.

8. **Watch the magic open up.** Here is where you'll begin to see life differently than you have before. You will begin to wonder how in the world you ever were the person you were years before. I call these tangible results, even though they are often mental results as well, only noticeable to you in how to feel about yourself and the

life you are building. Many, however, are tangible, *real* results – when you double your sales, when you lose 25 pounds, when you find yourself laughing louder and more often, or when you wake up at 5 a.m. with a smile on your face, excited for the day.

9. **Kick that growth into gear.** Get out of your comfort zone and you'll start to really feel good. Now you're in total charge and in that creative stage – a far cry from simply existing day to day. When you start going to bed on Sunday night with as much excitement as you feel at 5 p.m. on Friday, that's when you've made it.

10. **Now that you've made it, you have to keep it.** Don't get complacent or take your foot off the gas pedal. Many people get to a certain point – and feel a certain level of satisfaction – and tell themselves that they've 'made it,' which, in essence, they have. But in order to keep it, these new learned skills must stick with you. Keep going, keep growing and improving – always be more.

That's it, it's that simple. These are the foundations you'll need to start achieving your goals. Don't wait – jump in head-first and watch yourself reap the benefits. You'll be rewarded first with a sense of satisfaction that your boat is heading in the right direction, and it's just a matter of time before you hit new land. Then, from there, the rest of the feelings will flood in – accomplishment most of all.

Nothing will feel better than that feeling, knowing you have started your own journey to your own personal greatness.

Compound effect

Once you have started your climb up the mountain and started to see results, it is time to let the compound effect take hold and rocket you to new echelons of greatness.

The compound effect is the same as compound interest – it takes time to build up, but when it reaches a significant mass, something beautiful occurs. A multiplier kicks into gear and spurs you along the way.

Compound interest can be measured and calculated, but when life has a compound effect on you, it's a universal thing that is only measurable when you look at where you came from and compare it to where you are now. Once you have all your daily habits dialed in, and you've got a plan and have rid yourself of negativity, the universe has a remarkable way of taking care of everything else.

You've put in the hard work. Now it's time for your reward. Your energy will begin to attract the right kind of people and the right opportunities will present themselves. When you're happy, you'll notice more happy people, and if you stay disciplined, you'll have less and less time for unfocused, undisciplined people. Get in a great state of mind and your life's journey will be that much easier.

CHAPTER 12

THE MAGIC IS IN THE UNKNOWN

I magine, for a moment, that you could map out your life – from Point A, when you're a small child, to Point B, as a senior citizen – as if you were simply programming the GPS system in your car.

The computer would instinctively know exactly where you were in that moment at Point A – in grade school, or playing in a sandbox, or sleeping in a crib next to your parents' bed – and, once you punch in your final destination, out shoots a slew of directions and instructions, mapping out your next 80 years or so.

Every detail of your life, however small, would be there laid out before you. You'd know where to go, what girl to talk to, what classes to take in high school, what investments to make, which city to retire to, and so on. It would, no doubt, be a very comfortable existence – and a potentially lucrative one, if that GPS system happened to tell you which tech stocks to invest in, or on what team to lay a large Super Bowl wager.

You'd know, too, exactly how your professional life would shake out, thus ensuring every career move you make, and every business you start, is the correct choice.

But where's the fun in that? You'd be successful, sure, but wouldn't you find yourself bored? I know I would.

The phrase "it's the journey and not the destination" may be something of a tired cliché, but it's a well-worn phrase for a reason – because it's true. And the fact of the matter is this: We don't have a crystal ball – or a magic 8-ball or a GPS system for life – because we aren't supposed to have such things. That's not how this road trip we call life works.

We are not supposed to know how we are going to get where we're going, and we're certainly not supposed to know the route. We'd miss a lot of excellent side-trips and shortcuts if the opposite was true.

And if we knew how something was going to turn out in advance, there is a very real chance that we'd pass up on doing something. If you knew that you'd start a business that would ultimately fail, but you'd learn valuable lessons – and make important connections – along the way, would you still do it? Or, away from the office, if you knew your marriage would end in divorce, but you'd still get a couple amazing kids out of the union, would you still pop the question?

Conversely, what would you choose if you knew that a new venture would lead to success and wealth, but would be such a difficult journey to get there that you'd have second thoughts about it?

These are all tough-to-answer hypotheticals, and hypothetical is exactly how these quandaries should stay. We can't know the answer to these many questions before we start, so instead, we're left to our own belief in ourselves, and to faith – or, to quote the title of a more-than-200-years-old Italian opera: *La Forza del Destino*.

Which, roughly translated, means The Power of Fate.

To put it into a more practical metaphor, it's also a concept similar to driving across the country in the dark. You can turn your headlights on, and power 'em up as high as you'd like, but you still aren't going to be able to see all the way from Los Angeles to New York. Instead, you'll only be able to see about 50 feet in front of you. In reality, it's all you need.

As for the rest of the country? Well, you'll get there when you get there. In the meantime, you just have to trust that the next 50 feet will unfold just like the last 50 – or better.

Faith is the belief in the unknown, and an act of trusting that the process will get you what you need. And when you accept that faith – and fate – exist, and you start living in that reality, and in the comfort of knowing that the next 50 feet will be just fine, this is the beginning of true growth.

You will begin to see life differently, and you will see opportunities differently, and see your problems – big or small – with a different slant. The challenges that you once thought were obstacles? Now you'll see them as catapults forward and a new source of power and strength.

It's important to realize that quite often, when you get a little bit uncomfortable in life and stretch yourself to really "go after it" that is when you truly begin to reside in the lofty space where the world's most successful people hang out.

Successful people have made a living – and a life – out of enjoying the results of a journey that has, more often than not, involved plenty of risk. They're not afraid and act courageously yet with caution, act aggressively but with compassion, and make their moves from a position of strength while also showing a fragile side.

These successful people operate on inspiration, and though they face the same potential pitfalls as the rest of us – they don't have that magic 8-ball either – they also do not operate with excuses at the ready, nor any thoughts that they can't do it.

Don't be one of those people who never experience this type of bliss – the wave of adrenaline that comes with pushing all your chips into the middle of the table – simply because you are too afraid to explore the unknown.

Perhaps Martin Luther King, Jr. said it best: "Faith is taking the first step even when you don't see the whole staircase."

Take chances, move outside your comfort zone. Explore. This is where the real magic truly lies.

It goes against most peoples' inherent way of thinking, but it's important to take these chances and, in many cases, do the exact opposite of not just what others are doing, but what a section of your brain is telling you, too.

The ability to push through that risk-adverse part of your brain is why only a select few are truly successful, and why three percent of the population are said to control 96 percent of the world's wealth.

Successful people aren't afraid to move beyond their comfort zone, but for the average people, making a move can be incredibly difficult. It has always been this way and is, in large part, a survival instinct. It's worked into our DNA.

In fact, the idea that we are essentially "of two selves" is the key component of famed U.S. businessman and self-help author Napoleon Hill's greatest work. Hill, who published much of his work in the years surrounding the Great Depression, was of the mind that each individual has, within itself, two people. The first is the practical person, who – in modern times – is seen as the responsible one. The person who gets a good job, pays the bills on time, and makes conservative moves.

The second is quite the opposite. That self is the one that wants to take risks, be adventurous and risk it all (or at least some of it) for even more. The 'no pain, no gain' self, if you will.

There's one problem with this philosophy, of course – and you may have discovered it already: Taking these risks is difficult. If stepping out of your comfort zone was easy, everyone would do it.

I equate it to skydiving – something I recently did, despite what I long-perceived to be a fear of heights. Fear of heights or not, and with daredevils not included, I can tell you this: no matter how much you *want* to jump out of an airplane, it is awfully tough to actually step across the edge. It'd be much, much easier if you were pushed and had no choice.

And the same goes for pushing yourself into the realm of your other, risk-taking self.

It's a difficult step, no question about it. But consider that nearly every successful person – from Thomas Edison to Steve Jobs to Mark Zuckerberg – has forced him or herself to take that step, and it becomes slightly easier to rationalize.

But when you're ready to take this step, it will no doubt lead to the promised land – full of happiness and a renewed faith that you had no idea was inside of you this entire time. You'll smile more, be happier, laugh louder and have a life of abundance. But if you never take that step over the edge, you'll never know what was truly – potentially – in store for you. The only way to find out is to summon the strength and courage to step forward.

Even as I started to write this book, I had no clear idea about how I would achieve my ultimate goal – to be a top public speaker. I had no idea how I would go about becoming an author, either, but here I am. One word at a time, one sentence after another. It was the same process I undertook when I began training for triathlons. At the start, I had absolutely no idea how I would ever be able to swim 1.5 km or ride a bike for 160 km. All I had was a process and a plan, and I knew if I followed it, I'd eventually get to where I needed to be.

And now, I've done all those things I set out to achieve – and not because I knew years in advance that I'd be able to, but because back then, before I'd taken a single step forward, I visualized myself achieving those dreams, from speaking in front of a crowd to crossing the finish line after completing a grueling race.

No matter what unknown you are stepping into – whether it's thinking of moving your business in new direction or simply asking out that girl you like – you may know, deep down, that it will be very good for you. But you'll also be scared, and let me tell you, you are supposed to feel scared. You're supposed to be uncertain and second-guessing yourself. What you *shouldn't* do, however, is fill your head with negative thoughts and only imagine the negative outcomes. These are your true moments of inspiration that you need to tackle head-on, so let the positive feelings wash the negative thoughts to the side. Don't talk yourself out of these decisions, no matter what your body and soul tells you deep down in your core.

I believe that each of us has the power to overcome this penchant for safety, and – if we push past it – we all have the ability to change our lives, whether that means financially, personally, or otherwise.

Here is what I want you to do the next time inspiration hits: ignore, as best you can, the adrenaline that shoots through your body. This 'adrenaline dump' is always the first thing to occur in a "fight or flight" scenario. Don't give in to it. When you are experiencing a true defining moment, you will feel a much smaller transition of adrenaline, but the feeling is still there. Give yourself a few minutes to allow the adrenaline to flow through you and then explain to yourself how much better you'll feel if you were to take this leap and make this latest inspiration a part of your life.

Don't back down from it, and under no circumstance should you tell yourself anything negative about the opportunity for one full day. Try not to let any "I can't" thoughts even enter your mind. Then, after that 24-hour period is over, if you still find yourself wondering how much better your life would be if you took the risk-in-question, then it's clearly a leap worth making.

From there, take the next step towards it, whatever it may be. And from there, the next step, and then next. Stay focused on the 50 feet in front of you, and the next 50 and before you know it, you'll be clear across the country.

I've achieved much of what I've set out to do, and it's never been because I had any predictive powers – sorry, my crystal ball has been out of gas for awhile – but it's because I've made a conscious effort to live in the present. I've just enjoyed the journey – and the surprises that have come along – with faith in knowing that I'll make it to the finish line eventually.

And even if the end result isn't exactly how I pictured it might be, I'll have learned an awful lot about myself and grown as a person along the way. Place your focus on the process of getting to that goal and always remember, it's not reaching the goal that ultimately counts, it is about what you develop inside yourself that does.

Because while you're shooting for this goal, you are building new skills, learning to be disciplined, and forming habits of a champion. Once those habits are cemented within you, they're transferable to any future dream or endeavour and will serve you well in the long term.

My personal dream is rooted in helping others and being of service to them as they try to improve themselves and become successful. To me, motivating and trying to help people reach their best is something that comes naturally – the nexus of all my talents and skills aligned themselves and this goal to help was staring me right in the face. Next was the process, and I worked it for years, and in that time I discovered that I enjoyed writing and public speaking. And this is where I am today. Who would have ever thought? If you'd have asked me just three years ago, there is no way I'd have ever told you I'd be doing either of those two things. Not in a million years would those words come out of my mouth, but it was through following my process that I was shown the way, and sure enough, my future unfolded in front of me.

In those early stages, I told myself that the only way to become a polished speaker is to speak, and the only way to become a good writer is to write. So I did both. I just leapt in with both feet and worked on improving myself from the ground up.

What I didn't do is dwell on the negative and wonder "who would ever want to read my book?" or ask myself "Who, exactly, am I going to speak to?"

I have a friend, Marlene, who runs a senior's living facility, and one day, we were speaking about our jobs, and I said I was planning to write about my life, and speak to people. Wouldn't it be great, I said, if my first speaking engagement was at her seniors' home.

We laughed, and agreed that it would be a good idea – and make a great story. Now, if I had looked at it like many others might have, and asked myself why I'd bother speaking to a bunch of likely disinterested seniors – not exactly my target audience – then I'd never have even got started with my speaking journey. Because let's face it, unless you're selling out Carnegie Hall or Madison Square Garden, there's never going to be the perfect venue – the location will be wrong, the lighting will be off, or the audience too small.

Instead, I realized right away that this seniors' home – or anywhere else with four walls and an audience – would be just fine. I knew it would take years to hone my craft, and that I'd likely stumble along the way. I don't know how long that process will take – I still don't know – but I know that nothing is instant.

Maybe one day, I'll get to Carnegie Hall if I follow my "other self" along the way.

I also know that my positive traits – my confidence, my determination and my passion – will lead me in the right direction.

Passion begets passion. If you're not living passionately in all areas of your life, how can you logically expect to have a bright, passionate, exciting, successful future? These things you want – whatever they are – will not happen "just because." You have to work for them, and if you don't – if instead, you find yourself in something of an abyss of mediocrity – then it's time to make a change.

Change your routines – wake up earlier, be healthy, stick to a plan or a schedule. Eventually, you'll see measurable results.

By leaping into the unknown, there are going to be a few bumps and bruises along the way – ones you can't even conceive of in the beginning – but that's OK. Don't worry about it – believe me, nobody else will either. We tend to care far too much in today's world about how we look to other people, and we don't want others to see us fail. Perhaps it's an ego thing, or an embarrassment thing, who knows. Maybe it's combination of both. But if we do trip ourselves up, it's also worth it to just take the loss. Own it. Yes, maybe you failed, but you failed trying to do something awesome, and it didn't decrease your enthusiasm, so all is well.

It's simply temporary, and in the long run, it won't make the slightest difference. When you're standing at the top of a huge staircase, nobody remembers that you tripped over your shoelace on the third stair.

Of course, now that I've said all this about taking risks and pushing yourself beyond what part of your brain tells you is possible, it's important to note one more thing – it's key that you balance this idea of your two selves. If we leave the "other self" to its own devices, we're bound to take our life savings to the roulette table and bet it all on black. These are not the types of risks we're talking about – calculated, "smart" risk are entirely different. And as long as you remain in good standing with your two entities, and keep them balanced, you should be able to obtain every goal you have, and achieve every goal you set for yourself. What more could you hope for?

CHAPTER 13

FULL CIRCLE - THE BEST FOR LAST

From everything I have gathered, from the hundreds of books I have read, and from all the successful people I have spoken with and studied, I have discovered that the magic and true beauty of this process of bettering oneself lies in the end. There is one last chapter remaining once you have become successful in your endeavours and reached the top. It's time to give back and help other people understand the process and help them achieve their goals and dreams.

It takes years to be at peace in your mind, be in peak physical condition, have a joyous life, have a life full of passion and have a heart full of love. It takes great effort to have control of your life and mind. These are noble endeavours and reserved for those of us who take the time to focus on it and not settle for anything less.

Once you have achieved this state and are at the point in your life where love, money, success and peace are flowing, you have entered this final chapter. Yes, your success to date has resulted in a great lifestyle – maybe you've got nice cars, a nice home, a collection of great wine and you only dine at the finest of restaurants. That's great – it truly is - but the best is yet to come.

Now you get to help other people. Based on everything I have learned to date, this is the best part. This is the part that will bring you the most satisfaction, believe me. There is one thing that almost every successful person has in common and that is that they have a love of helping others. Ask Rick Hansen and he will tell you. Or ask Bill Gates, a charitable man who has given away 100 times more money than most of us will ever even earn.

This help comes in many forms. It can be showing someone how to forgive and love again. Or maybe you give back by volunteering, or donating to charity, or by helping people who are in mental anguish, who are hungry or cold, or maybe you'll go build schools in Africa. Whatever you do, you will be setting a great example for those people around you. The best part is that *you* get to pick how you give back. We all seem to assume that the only way to give is to give money. Money is great – and there's no shortage of good causes that could use a few dollars – but there are other ways to help, too. You can give your heart to someone. You can give a smile, hold open a door, be kind, play with a child, support your aging parents, give time to your church, or coach a sport in your community. The list goes on.

We spend most of our lives taking, and if we don't complete the circle by giving back we will be left at the end wondering what it all was about. What was the point? We know that we can't take our worldly possessions to the grave, but it is what we leave behind that becomes our legacy.

"Being the richest man in the cemetery, doesn't matter to me. Going to bed at night saying we've done something wonderful, that's what matters to me."

— Steve Jobs

As we take these final steps on our journey together, I want to invite you to think about what you are most passionate about in this world. What do you care for most deeply? What excites you? What legacy would light you up? What could you do today that would make you proud? What action could you take that would be a signal to your own spirit that your life is being lived well? And if you were truly inspired, what would you like to give or create?

All of these questions bring us close to the true meaning of wealth: THE SECRET TO LIVING IS GIVING.

It can be giving of your emotions; giving your presence to your kids, to your family, to your husband or your wife, to your friends, your associates. Our work is also our gift, and we all have something to give. In fact, after love, the most valuable gift we can give is our labour. Volunteering our time, giving our unique level of caring, and sharing our skills will also give you significant "returns."

There is nothing like the power of the human soul on fire. Along the way, human caring touched me, as did the books I read. I was transported from a world of limitations to a life of endless possibility as I entered the minds of authors who had already transformed their lives. There is no way that you will learn and understand the messages of the universe and the wise without reading about them. It takes time to make the best you. You can make a fantastic version of yourself if you want to take the time to get inside your own head and explore how you think. It will take some time to understand and manage the neural connections that make up you. You see, the mind is like a wild animal, if you let it run wild, it will be wild. Let there be no question about this. It will run all over the place. You must take the time to study yourself and ask yourself the real, tough questions. Who do I want to be? How do I want to behave? How do I want to speak? What am I passionate about? What changes can I make? How can I impact others?

Once you have a framework to these questions, get to work! Immerse yourself in books, slow down your mind, exercise, sleep well, have great friends who uplift you, work hard, have a positive outlook, laugh your ass off, love your family, help others, give back and live a large life. Always remember that **inner happiness is the fuel for success.**

The human mind is an amazing thing. It has a built-in survival mechanism, so it tends to look for what is wrong, what to avoid, what to look out for, and what could go wrong. You may have evolved, but your brain is still a million-year old structure. You want to be fulfilled and happy, but that is not the brain's first priority. **You have to take control of it.**

You see, to get the true rewards from life you must work at it. Start working right now, there is no better time. I don't care if you are 10 years old or 70 – get going. The rewards or returns you will realize from gaining control over your mind and thoughts will be fantastic. No longer will the outside environment, other people's words, the weather, or the day of the week control you. Your eyes will open wide, your soul will blossom and you will receive the inheritance we are promised. That is, peace of mind, joy, wealth and happiness on a regular basis.

"Believe in yourself. Focus on what you want. Think big. Set goals. Do what excites you. Visualize positive outcomes. Do everything with love. Make time to relax. Enjoy life. Be crazy. Be weird. Choose empowering beliefs. Feed your mind and your body with good things. Meditate. Be grateful for what you have. Be kind. Don't compare yourself to others. Be honest. Work hard. Work smart. Find your purpose. Invest in yourself. Practice positive self-talk. Get your priorities straight. Never give up."

— Bruce Ellemo

ABOUT THE AUTHOR

Bruce Ellemo, a father of two and former three-time All-Canadian soccer player, holds a degree in economics from the University of Victoria. As founder and president of his company, www.assuredlease.com, Bruce has negotiated over $100-million in lease finance transactions across Canada and the United States.

Through his study of many of our greatest modern-life philosophers - including Earl Nightingale, Jim Rohn, Dr. Wayne Dyer, Napoleon Hill, Steven Covey and Deepak Chopra, to name a few – and his business negotiations over the last 20 years, Bruce has been able to develop a deepened ability to understand himself and the people with whom he does business. Through this, he has built and maintained strong relationships with some of the largest equipment manufacturers in North America for over 20 years. Bruce's specialty lies in finding creative business solutions that work for small-business owners as well as large corporations.

In his spare time, Bruce enjoys golfing, boating, skiing, logging a few miles on his road-bike, going to the gym and spending time with his family.